THERE'S SO MUCH MORE!

After scouring through thousands of hours of footage spanning more than two decades, the **Art Williams Best** video team has assembled the purest, most comprehensive collection of Art Williams' wisdom on winning in business and life.

Use this QR code to transport you directly to the ArtWilliamsBest Youtube Channel where you will find more than 150 videos, each carefully crafted to distill the essence of Art's no nonsense philosophy on building a business that lasts, investing in people to grow unstoppable teams and building wealth to impact future generations.

Welcome to Art Williams Best!

THE A.L. WILLIAMS WAY

By

ART WILLIAMS

ISBN: 979-8-9899986-6-1 (Paperback)
979-8-9899986-7-8 (eBook)

Published by:
Art Williams Best

Opening Thoughts

It is important that the people of A.L. Williams NEVER FORGET the PRINCIPLES and TRADITIONS that our company was founded upon. I believe we are unique in American business because it is not only important THAT we win, it is important HOW we win. We are unique because of our commitment to DOING WHATS RIGHT for the consumer and DELIVERING ON OUR COMMITMENTS to our people.

The Spirit of A.L. Williams

When A.L. Williams was founded on February 10, 1977, we didn't have a lot going for us in the traditional sense. We had no money, no administration, little support – not even a name! What we DID HAVE was A CONCEPT that was right for the consumer. We also had A DREAM that one day A.L. Williams would become one of the most famous companies in America – number one in our industry, that A.L. Williams would change the direction and thinking of the largest industry in the world, that our leaders would become the most successful people in American business and that we would take our top people to all the great places in the world. Those seemed like impossible goals to everyone but the "Original 85."

Those early pioneers had a special kind of SPIRIT. Throughout the proud history of A.L. Williams, that spirit has endured. In fact, I believe the "SPIRIT OF A.L. WILLIAMS" is the GLUE that holds our company together.

It is the DUTY AND RESPONSIBILITY of every A.L. Williams person TO NEVER FORGET our history, TO NEVER CHANGE those special things that make us different and unique AND to NEVER LOSE THE SPIRIT of A.L. Williams. This is MORE than a business to every red-blooded A.L. Williams person.

Trust Your Instincts and Your Feelings

When I was doing recruiting interviews, Opportunity Meetings and Fast Start Schools, the first thing I always told everyone was, "Don't worry about the numbers or technical aspects of A.L. Williams." Anyone can learn the mechanics of the business. All that takes is a little time and effort. The key to being successful at A.L. Williams is feeling good about what we do. You've got to feel good about the kind of people we are, the way we talk, the way we dress, the way we act, everything.

Follow Your Instincts

If your instincts say to you, "I like these people, I like what they do, I believe I could get excited about this this is my kind of company" -then and only then should you join us. If you don't have those feelings, stay away – for you will only be disappointed.

Always remember:

The difference in a $100,000 a year salesperson and a $5,000 a year salesperson is one thing-THE WAY THEY FEEL ABOUT WHAT THEY DO.

It always amazed me that two people could join A.L. Williams, attend the same training classes, sell the same products, have the same position, give the same presentation -yet one would fail and one would be excited and successful. I finally realized that the difference was THE WAY THEY FELT ABOUT WHAT THEY DID.

I believe that, if you're only excited about the money you can make, you will surely fail. If you recruit and sell the financial opportunity only, you will surely fail. The reason is that when you have disappointments (and everyone will have someone tell them no, etc.), you will get discouraged because the money always comes later, AFTER you pick up policies, AFTER you make a sale, AFTER you get your promotion and AFTER you recruit someone that gets licensed, learns the business and makes a sale.

You must feel good about the A.L. Williams Way. Those feelings are THE FIRST STEP TO GREATNESS.

My primary purpose in writing The A.L. Williams Way is to have you understand our wonderful company and the way we do business. I believe there are “only two things” you must have to see your “dreams come true” at A.L. Williams.

No. 1 - You must feel good about A.L. Williams and the things we stand for; and
No. 2 - You must be able to get others (clients and recruits) to feel the same way.

If you can achieve those two things, there will be no stopping you. You will have success professionally, financially, and personally beyond your wildest imagination.

Now, let’s discover the A.L. Williams Way!!

Table of Contents

Our Uniqueness

How To Win

Build People, Not Sales

Leadership Attitude

Leadership Responsibilities

The Partners In A.L. Williams

Business Principles

OUR UNIQUENESS

IN THIS SECTION:

- Our Uniqueness
- Built for a Different Kind of People
- A Definite Philosophy
- A Sales Company
- A New Concept for Sales
- The Replacement Concept
- A Positive "Can Do" Attitude
- The Human Factor
- A Chance to Do Something Special
- A Better Way to Build a Company
- Involving Spouses in Business Life
- A Controversial Company
- Scoreboard
- 1985 National Champs
- Fastest Growing Company
- We Are Different From Our Competition
- The War Is On
- Be Part of a Winner
- Our System Saves Money for the Consumer
- Can All These be Wrong

Our Uniqueness

"In 1977, we didn't know "nothing about nothing" when it came to building a company in the traditional sense of the word. But we believed that you had to be right. You had to do what was right for consumers and for the salespeople. And, we knew that people were tired of the way things had been done in the traditional industry. We wanted to feel good about our company and our products -it was our friends, our communities and our families that we would serve.

"We didn't have the kind of management sophistication that you get at Harvard. All we had was our own years of experience in the industry and just plain old common sense. We asked ourselves how we would like to be treated. We put ourselves in the place of the consumer and tried to consider what was the best product for our families -and that's the product we decided to sell. We didn't choose the product that could make the company the most money or us the most money, but we chose the product that was best for consumers.

"And that's the way we started A.L. Williams."

—Art Williams

Built for a Different Kind of People

"There has never been a test -
and there never will be a test -
that can measure the heart of a man or woman."
—Art Williams

People are a company's **greatest asset.**

Most corporations in America have been influenced too much by things like college degrees, college board scores, IQ, background and family status.

A.L. Williams believes that "inside" qualities are far more important than those kinds of "outside" qualities. I believe that you never know what people are made of until you give them a chance out on the playing field.

A.L. Williams believes that every red-blooded American, man or woman, wants to be somebody. We were built to give these people – the people who have been "locked out" of corporate America or locked out of the opportunity to go into business for themselves – a chance to stand on their own two feet, a chance to go into business for themselves and do something special with their lives.

We are able to attract a different kind of person to the business community, a person who wants to be somebody who still knows how to dream, who can still hope, who is willing to fight for what he or she believes is right – the kind of person who is the heart and soul of America.

A. L. Williams people are not "corporate executive" types – and we're proud of it!

A Definite Philosophy

"At A.L. Williams, we stand for something, and we won't change."
—Art Williams

Most people today have a feeling that corporate America doesn't care about quality or about doing what's right – that they're only interested in making a profit.

Before we ever made our first sale, A.L. Williams looked at what was available to the consumer. We found that cash value life insurance was NOT the best way to provide protection for families. We discovered that the best way was a simple little philosophy of "BUY TERM AND INVEST THE DIFFERENCE."

We made "buy term and invest the difference" the cornerstone of our philosophy.

We were going to sell the consumer what was best; we were going to sell him what we believed in owning on our own lives. And we were going to do that 100% of the time. You can't fool the consumer forever. If you don't do what's right, you might get by for one day, one week, one month or one year – but sooner or later, he'll smell you out.

Most companies sell dozens of different products; if you don't like one, they'll offer you another. We sell ONE PRODUCT ALL THE TIME -BECAUSE IT'S THE RIGHT PRODUCT!

One thing I've learned in business is that the American consumer hates a "mealymouth" or a "fencesitter" – an individual or company that doesn't have a firm, committed belief in certain values.

At A.L. Williams, we don't change our mind or change our products depending on which way the winds blow in the insurance industry. The only changes we make are those that make our products better first for the consumer, second for the field force and third for the company – in that order.

A Sales Company

"A.L. Williams is a company built by salespeople, for salespeople."
—Art Williams

In 1977, when we founded A.L. Williams, we adopted the motto: "A.L. Williams is a company where salespeople are 'KING.' " Most businesses in America are run by lawyers, accountants, actuaries or business school graduates.

When this company was formed, we made the decision that unless you've carried a briefcase in the field, unless you know what it's like out there in the real world, unless you've experienced "first hand" what this company is all about, you're not going to have any say-so in affecting the lives of the salespeople.

In any sales company, it is the salespeople who take the biggest chance. They are out there "bustin' it" EVERY DAY: they're fighting the competition on the front lines and living on commission income. THEY DESERVE THE GREATEST FINANCIAL REWARDS!

In a great company, you put the concerns of the people before the concerns of profitability. Because if you take care of your people, the profits will, come. At A.L. Williams, our salespeople are the most important asset we have. We've built our company around that belief. We believe that's one of the KEYS to our incredtble success.

A New Concept For Sales

"A.L. Williams' system of 'sales management' takes the 'gotcbas' out of living on commission income."
—Art Williams

The good thing about sales is that you can control your own income. If you want to work twice as hard, sell twice as much, you can make twice as much money.

The bad thing about sales is that it is a terribly insecure profession. Salespeople are unemployed every day! If you don't go out and beat the bushes for prospects every day, you don't eat.

We believe that you go into business for yourself to build not only a good income, but a secure income. But real security is missing from traditional sales jobs.

We took the best thing from sales, which is commissions, where you can control your own income, and we added to it a management concept called "sales management," where you can build an organization and override large numbers of people. Through sales management, you have the ability to build not only a big income, but a secure income, as well.

With sales management, you can get sick and not have it destroy your business. You can take a vacation without going broke. Sales management is the key to peace of mind and security for salespeople.

The Replacement Concept

"Our replacement concept frees people to hire the best people they can find, without the traditional 'corporate' fear of being left standing on the corporate ladder."
—Art Williams

In most corporations, you live in fear of ever recruiting or hiring someone who's as good or better than you are.

There are usually just a few positions at the top, and if you participate in that race up the corporate ladder, you live in fear that somebody's going to pass you up. You're safer to hire people who are not so good or try to hold back good people, but that, in turn, hurts your business.

A. L. Williams came up with a replacement concept that eliminates that fear. In A.L. Williams, there are an unlimited number of top level positions. And by hiring and developing good people, anyone can earn promotions. In a sense, a person in A.L. Williams improves his chances for success when he develops a person "to take his place" at each management level. It's to the advantage of the person who hires you to make sure you do well or better than he does.

Finally, in our business world, we've created an environment where a person is encouraged to hire the best people he can find, without fear. And, in turn, he can succeed as much as his talents allow without fearing that he will be held back.

The replacement concept in sales management is a totally new concept in the corporate world. AND IT WORKS!

A Positive "Can Do" Attitude

"From day one, we never had any doubt that we'd be the greatest success story in American business. We know how to make things happen – and were doing it!"
—Art Williams

Corporate America, over the last 10 years, has struggled like never before. Companies have complained about foreign competition, about the economy, about the oil crisis, and so on. They've made all kinds of excuses for why their business was not growing and improving.

A.L. Williams is positive and excited about the future of this country and the future of A.L Williams. We think our leaders are going to "do it bigger" and make more money than ever before. We won't be intimidated by competition. Those things are a part of the free enterprise system and we re confident that we can succeed in that system. WE EXPECT TO WIN!

A.L. Williams is the kind of company that people want to join. Nobody wants to join a company that has given up, that feels like its best days are over.

At A.L Williams, we've accomplished incredible things, and we know that we're going to get better and better and be more and more successful in the future. We're not planningto go backward. and we won't – because we know we can MAKE THINGS HAPPEN.

The Human Factor

"A.L. Williams will always consider 'the human factor' in every business decision."
—Art Williams

Many corporations spend more time and money keeping their computers working and their offices clean than meeting the needs of the consumer or the needs of their people.

We believe that people ARE the company and how you treat those people will determine your success or failure as a company. And, we believe that a company's first commitment is to the people it serves -the consumer. It is the consumer who will buy – or not buy – your product. How a company feels about the consumer will determine whether or not it will be successful.

The insurance industry has made a particularly bad impression with the consumer. Most folks will cross the street to avoid talking to an insurance salesman. WE DON'T WANT THAT IMAGE IN OUR COMPANY: we don't want to be like "insurance salespeople" or "traditional salespeople."

A.L.. Williams believes in "treating people good" in building a sales force. We don't believe in using threats and intimidation tactics in dealing with our people. Most business schools teach their people that you shouldn't get close to your people; that you must let everyone know who his "boss" is at all times. In A.L. Williams, we don't believe you can lead people unless you get to know them and care about them. You have to get emotionally involved with them. A leader's job is to help people achieve their goals. A.L. Williams is a team where EVERYONE CARES ABOUT EVERYBODY.

A Chance to Do Something Special

"At A.L. Williams we recruit from Middle America, 'average' people who have the heart of a champion."
—Art Williams

At A.L. Williams, we give average, ordinary people a chance to build a business they are proud of and to gain financial independence for themselves and their families.

We take people who have "heart" and "drive," who want to do something great with their lives, and we give them the opportunity to dream again, set goals and be what they are capable of being.

If you come to work for us, we don't care what you look like, what your education and background are. We're going to give you a chance to become financially independent, to have the kind of life most people only dream about, and to accomplish something great in the free enterprise system.

At A.L. Williams, you can work full-time and "go for it" all the way, or you can work parttime and earn that extra income that can make the difference for your family between just getting by and having a comfortable life.

No other company in America offers the business opportunity that we offer to Middle American people. We believe that the only qualifications for success are a "burning desire" to succeed and a "will to win.

If you've got those two qualities, we want you in A.L. Williams.

A Better Way to Build a Company

"The key to success in the free enterprise system is getting a quality product to the customer at a cheaper cost. We've done that at A.L. Williams."
—Art Williams

A.L. Williams has two unique competitive advantages:

No. 1 - We save people money.

Most companies are product-oriented. They go out there to sell a product to the consumer, to get the consumer to spend more money.

The American consumer today is more concerned, more frustrated about his personal financial situation than ever before. We go into a home to save people money. We go in to give people more value for their money. We don't sell policies.

No. 2 - We champion the cause of part-timers.

By championing the cause of part-timers we found a way to recruit a better quality of person into this industry, and also found a more efficient way to get the product to the consumer.

Better people: Most people can't see themselves selling anything, especially insurance. Plus, in the insurance industry, the turn-over rate is 80-90%. Most people don't make it. You can't expect someone with family responsibilities to take a chance like that.

Yet, almost everybody needs extra income. With our part-time position, there's no risk to coming part-time. We can hire a better quality person, a family person, a person who's known in the community -instead of the "typical salesman" type.

More efficient: Our competition spends thousands of dollars supporting people who won't stay in the business. Our part-time people already have the stability of a full-time income. They make a commission through their part-time sales, and never threaten the security of their family while they're learning the business.

Many of our competitors spend millions of dollars advertising on TV and in the papers. we don't do that. We deal with our clients face-to-face through our part-timers.

We don't have to advertise. And, we don t have those huge costs to pass on to the consumer.

Involving Spouses in Business Life

'A.L. Williams believes that a husband and wife, in partnership in business, working together to be successful, can accomplish more than any four or five individuals."
—Art Williams

Corporate America frowns on getting the spouse involved in the business. They are "left out" of meetings and conventions or other company events. They are outsiders in their partner's business life.

At A.L. Williams, we never have a convention, sales meeting, management meeting, or anything else, without encouraging the spouse to attend. We want the spouses of our salespeople to KNOW our concepts and beliefs: we want them to know what this company is all about. And, most important, we want them to know that this is THEIR business, as well as their spouse's.

We recognize that an involved, supportive spouse is the strongest asset that any individual could have. If the spouse understands and supports the business goals of his or her partner, the individual has a more positive attitude, a stronger commitment and higher confidence and self-esteem. Spouse involvement creates a powerful bond of communication and motivation that can provide many riches to the business life of any person.

We believe that a "team spirit" in the home is the foundation of great business success. Growth together as a couple involves growing together in all areas of one's life.

A Controversial Company

"Any company that tries to do something new, something unique in the American business community is going to be 'shot at' like you can't believe. That's OK with us we're controversial and proud of it!"

—Art Williams

Most companies are scared to "stick their heads up" and do something big. They're afraid to do anything that might be a little controversial. We know that to do something great, you've got to take a stand, and you can't be afraid of the results of taking a position. At this company, we want to do something great. We want to be a trendsetter, we want to revolutionize the largest, most powerful industry in the world. We want to change the direction of the life insurance industry because we mow that we have a better way. We want to be one of the most successful and dynamic companies in all of American business.

We also want our people to be among the most outstanding and the most successful business leaders in their communities. If you're going to do anything big, you're going to be controversial-and we ARE controversial. THE ALTERNATIVE to being controversial is to be average and ordinary.

We ain't average and ordinary!

Scoreboard

"Talk is cheap. You have to look at the scoreboard to get the facts."

—Art Williams

Every company in our industry "talks a good game." All companies make BIG PROMISES and BOLD PREDICTIONS. But it's WHAT'S ON THE SCOREBOARD THAT COUNTS. It's easy to talk a good game, anyone can talk. But you have to look at the Scoreboard to see if what is being said is FACT or JUST TALK .. to see if they did deliver ... if they did do what's right ... if they did win.

A.L. Williams Scoreboard

Born February 10, 1977, into one of the LARGEST INDUSTRIES in the world ... the top companies are among THE MOST FAMOUS NAMES in all business ... many of.these companies are OVER 100 YEARS OLD.

In our 7th year (1984), A.L. Williams became THE NATIONAL CHAMPIONS and we've been there ever since. Look at THE SCOREBOARD. A.L. Williams has done things that were once thought to be impossible.

But the thing that really stands out as our legacy: we won, we won big, and we won with class (by doing what's right).

1984-85 National Champs

In seven short years, we became No. 1 -incredible!

1985: $65.5 Billion

Superior MILICO products and the people-oriented A.L. Williams sales force are an unbeatable combination. It only makes sense that you would feel more comfortable with your future in the hands of the industry leader.

Fastest Growing Company

- They looked at the MILICO product.
- They learned about "Buy Term and Invest the Difference."
- They made the "Common Sense" choice.

A.L. Williams Production 1977-1985

(Face amount of policies placed in force from A.L. Williams sales - millions)

1977 - $317
1978 - $486
1979 - $1,198
1980 - $4,078
1981 - $6,658
1982 - $10,378
1983 - $24,000
1984 - $38,324
1985 - $65,591

It all started with 85 people. Eight years later, there were over 100,000- the largest sales force in the industry. For two consecutive years we have been national champions!

We Are Different From Our Competition

We found a better way to build a company. We hire better quality people.

When you're dealing with A.L. Williams, there are no high-pressure sales tactics. There are no gimmicks.

We're in the people business, and our first concern is the consumer.

That's what separates us from the competition!

That's why the American public puts insurance salesmen in the same class with used car salesmen ...

(Gallup poll lists Insurance sales as third from the bottom of the list in a 1981 poll)

"The War Is On."

First it was the cola wars.

Then it was the burger wars.

Competition is what makes the free enterprise system go. At A.L. Williams we welcome competition. W'e became No. 1 because we were not afraid to compete and because we delivered for the American consumer.

We accept the challenge of any company that wants to see if they are good enough to knock us off the top.

We're confident that everything is in place for us to dominate our industry for the next 20 to 25 years.

Bring 'em on!

Now it's the Insurance War.

To the competition: Beware!

You're not going to beat us with cheap talk and a slick public relations campaign. You're going to have to beat us in the marketplace by doing what's best for the consumer.

Buy term and invest the difference in an IRA is the best concept available today for Middle America.

Who's the No. 1 producer of term insurance?

We are.

Who's committed to selling term insurance 100% of the time?

We are.

Who's the leading spokesman of buy term and invest the difference?

We are.

Who's the company doing the job for the consumer?

We are.

Only pansies are scared to compete. The war is on, and we take no prisoners.

Be Part of a Winner

State of the Company 1986 Elcellent in all these categories

- Products
- Commissions
- Cash-Flow Potential
- RVP Deferred Renew
- MILICO Administration
- ALW Home Office Support
- Financial Support
- Communications
- Quality of Business
- National Image
- Regulatory Environment
- Management Experience
- Leader's Mental Toughness
- Marketing Tools
- American Can/ ALW Relationship
- Sales Force Attitudes
- Home Office Attitudes
- Fundamentals (Sales Force)
- Prospecting System (Referrals)

Big League Success
A.L. Williams Corporation
Motivation
Intangibles
Recruiting
Sales
Our Competition
The Future

Our System Saves Money for the Consumer

Developing a large network of independent men and women, we have eliminated the costly company expenses of maintaining and training the sales force.

We don't believe in national, mass-media advertising. Our philosophy calls for introducing our product one-on-one, across the kitchen table. That cuts tremendous advertising expenses which would have to be passed on to the consumer.

Our home office operates more efficiently than any in the business. The average industry's Administrative cost is seven employees for every $100 million of insurance. MILICO's Administrative cost is less than one employee for every $100 million of insurance.

Look at how MILICO stacks up against the competition ...

Number of employees per every $100 million of insurance in force.

MILICO Wins! Lowest employee number per $100 million insurance policys sold!

...as reported in The Chicago Tribune.

Can All These be Wrong?

These hard-hitting facts and data expose the myths of cash value as a savings program:

1877 "Traps Baited With Orphans" Elizur W'right
1901 "The Economic Theory of Risk and Insurance" Allan H. Willett
1905 "Business of Life Insurance" O.P.
1906 "How To Buy Life Insurance" O.P.
1907 "The Story of Life Insurance" Burton J. Hendrick
1916 "Life Insurance For Professors" Univ. of Calif. Publications in Economics, Vol. 4, No. 2

1917 "A License To Steal" Philander Banister Armstrong
1925 "Life Insurance Digest" Robert M. Messick
1929 "Life Insurance Simplified" Lewis R. Tebbetts
1930 "The Money Value of a Man" L.I. Dublin and A.]. Lotka
1933 "How Safe Is Life Insurance?" L. Seth Schnitman
1934 "Your Insurance" S.B. Cyzio
1936 "Life Insurance, A Critical Examination" Edward Berman
"Your Life Insurance and W11at to Do About It" David Gilbert and Jim Sullivan
"Life Insurance, A Legalized Racket" Mort Gilbert and E. Albert Gilbert
1938 "Life Insurance, America's Greatest Confidence Game" J.D. Kidder
"Life Insurance - Investing in Disaster" Mort & E.A. Gilbert
"Life Insurance Exposed" Daniel D. White
"Gouge" John Franklin Gaskill
1944 "You Pay and You Pay"
1946 "A Century of American Life Insurance" S.B. Clough
1947 "How to Buy Life Insurance" Phillip Gordis
1948 "Insurance and Your Security" E. Albert Gilbert

1952 "Personal Estate Planning in A Changing World" Rene Wormser

"Personal Finance and Investment" Wilford J. Eitman

1955 "Insurance W'ithout Exploitation" Edwin C. Guillet

"Your Insurance and How to Profit By It" Michael H. Levy

"Life Insurance From the Buyer's Point of View" 1955-68 Bureau of Econ. Research

1958 "The Grim Truth About Life Insurance" Ralph Hendershot

"Your Pocketbook Is Leaking" KP. Chartier

1960 "Common Cents in Investments and Insurance" Gerald Fitzgerald

"Vice President in Charge of Revolution" Murray Lincoln

1961 "Behind the Fine Print" Gayle E. Richardson

"Money You Can Keep" David Gilbert

1962 "Life Insurance, A Study in Delusion" Dennis L. Anderson

"Use and Abuse of Statistics" W.J. Reichmann

1963 "A View of Life Insurance" Wayne C. Knigge

"What's Wrong with Your Life Insurance" Norman F. Dacey

1964 "Life Insurance- Benefit or Fraud?"J. J. Brown

1965 "Life Insurance" Graduate School of Business, Indiana Univ.

1966 "The Great Misconceptions" Natl. Analytical Service, Inc.

"The Retail Price Structure in American Life Ins." Joseph M. Beth

"This Is Wbere Your Money Goes" Robert F. Kahroff

"Pay Now, Die Later" James Gollen

1967 "Why Waste Your Money on Life Insurance" J.E. Stowers

"The Consumer Union Report on Life Insurance"

"A Report on Life Insurance"

"A Study of Mutual Life Insurance Dividends" Frank Mcintosh

1968 "Houston Law Review" Randal A. Hendricks

"How to Avoid Being Overcharged by Your Life Insurance Salesman" Pawlick

"The Mortality Merchants" G. Scott Reynolds

1969 "The Life Book of Family Finance" Time-Life Books

"Stop Wasting Your Insurance Dollars" Dave Goodwin

1970 "Consumers Guide to Insurance Buying" Vladamir P. Chernik- Changing Times

1971 "Getting All the Life Insurance You're Paying For?" Thomas McSwain, M.D.

"How to Pay Lots Less for Life Insurance" Max Fogiel - Moneysworth

1974 "Consumer Report" Jan., Feb., March

"Term or Straight - Which Is Best for You?" Everybody's Money, Spring

"Let's Understand Life Insurance" Consumers Digest July/ Aug.

"The Bottom Line -A Little Straight Talk About Life Insurance" Dirks/ Grass - Playboy, May '74

1975 Congressional Record- July 8, 1975, Senator Phillip Hart

"The Consumer's Guide to Life Insurance" J. Tracy Oehlbeck

"How to Save Money on Your Life Insurance" Natl. Assn. for Truth In Life Ins.

1976 "The Search For the Hidden Treasure" Mitchell Educational Services, Inc.

1977 "Where Women Should Invest Money" Venita Van Caspel

"What's Happening to Life Insurance Dividends?" Consumer Report, March '77

"The Consumers Union Report on Life Insurance" 1977 Edition

"Dreams of Immortality" Max Apple - Mother Jones Magazine

1978 "Life Insurance: Myths and Facts" Consumer Digest Nov./Dec.

"False Advertising" Howard J. Ruff, The Ruff Times, Oct. 15

"Must Replacement Be A Dirty Dirty Word?" The Natl. Underwriter, Oct. 7

"Dollars & Sense" C. & . Associates

"The New Money Dynamics" Venita Van Caspel

"The 250 Billion Dollar Consumer Problem?" (Cash Value Life Ins.) J.V. Pruitt

"If You Need Help in Planning Your Finances" U.S. News and World Report

1979 "Insurance Industry Feels the Federal Lash" U.S. News & World Report, April

1981 "How Your Life Insurance Policies Rob You" Arthur Milton

1982 "How Life Insurance Companies Rob You" Walter S. Kenton, Jr.

1983 "Common Sense," by Art Williams, Parklake Publishers

"Tell Yesterday Goodbye: Time to Free 150 Million Americans From Their Life Insurance Trap" Arthur Milton

"Insurance: Costly Enigma" Washington Post

"Whole Life Is A Losing Game" Seattle Post Intelligence

1984 "The Disadvantages of W'hole Life Insurance Policies" William Doyle, Atlanta Constitution

"Inflation Keeps Cutting Value of Life Insurance Coverage" The Arizona Republic

"Universal Life: After 5 Years, Critics Say Confusion Persists" The Atlanta Journal

"The Peril in Financial Services" Business Week

"Straight Talk:" Princeton Information Corp.

"Power Phrases: Fact or Fantasy?"

"Variable Life: Just How New Is It"

"Run-Down On Those 'New' Products: Traditional Whole Life, Universal Life, Variable Life and Variable Universal Life"

"Universal Life - Coming Or Going"

1985 "Universal Life, It's Not the Answer" Art Williams

"Whole Life Insurance" Bill Doyle, Newark Star-Ledger

"IRA Warning: Stay Away From Whole Life Policies" SELF Magazine, February 1985

"Only Survivor of Tax Reforms: Term Insurance?" Richard Gilman, The National Underwriter

"Buy Policies for Life Insurance, Not for Investments" Bill Doyle, The Detroit News

"Tax Plan No Threat to Term Life Policy" William Doyle, The Atlanta Journal & The Atlanta Constitution

"Straight Talk:" "Treasury Tackles Life Insurance"

"Universal Life Up-Date"

"How Much Commission Is Enough?"

"U.S. Federal Trade Commission Statement" before Committee on Innerstate and Foreign Commerce, House of Representatives, U.S.

Contree by Dr. Albert Kramer Director, Bureau of Consumer Affairs of the F.T.C.

"Is Life Insurance Worth It" Maxwell S. Stewart

"Life Insurance and Annuities From Buyer's Point of View" Wm. Matteson

OTHERS

"A Formula for Financial Independence" Wm. A. Rudd

"Why Your Insurance Costs Too Much" Bernard J. Koerselman

"Life Insurance - Guide Planning and Buying" Editors of Consumer Reports

"Squeeze It Till the Eagle Grins" Scott Burns

HOW TO WIN

IN THIS SECTION:

- How to Win
- The A.L. Williams Image
- Reputation
- A Company Within a Company
- Prestige vs. Opportunity
- RVP Responsibility
- Time is the Key
- Prospecting the A.L. Williams Way
- Fundamentals of Prospecting
- Recruit's Natural Market
- Recruiting
- Our Recruiting Concept
- Be Careful Recruiting Salespeople
- Personal Profile
- The Sales Process
- Keys to Selling the A.L. Williams Way
- Field Training

- A Winning Presentation
- Keys to Making A Winning Presentation
- Referrals
- Prospecting with the “Form Method”
- Other Ways to Prospect
- Base Shop Guidelines
- Base Shop “Standard of Excellence”
- 150-Mile Rule
- Opening an Office
- Clustering
- Super Clustering
- “Ideal” RVP Office Setting
- Fast Start Schools
- Example of a Super Fast Start School
- Manager (Full-Timers) Meeting
- Training Sessions
- No “Gotchas”

How to Win

"If you are ever faced with making management decisions based on how they effect you, you will never be a great leader!"
—Art Williams

Over and over I see PANIC MANAGEMENT destroy more careers than almostanything I know of. There are three WEAKNESSES that cause a leader to panic.

No. 1 - Lack of activity

This is a numbers business.

No. 2 - A poor personal financial situation

It's not how much you make, but how much you keep that counts.

No. 3 - No definite system

You must have A SYSTEM.

You must take care of No. 1 and No. 2 "all by yourself." (No one can help you.) But if you MASTER THE PRINCIPLES in this chapter (How to Win), you will never be forced to panic because you will have "The Best System."

The A.L. Williams Image

"A leader must look like a winner, talk like a winner, act like a winner and be a winner."
—Art Williams

No. 1 - Dress conservatively

Men:

- No excessive jewelry
  (Example: Gold chains, diamond rings, and so on.)
- No flamboyant clothes
  (Example: Hats, shirts that draw attention, etc.)

- No long hair

Women:

- Look like a businessperson.

No. 2 - No alcohol served at any A.L. Williams meeting, convention, etc.
No. 3 - No excessive offices

- We make money in the field, not in the office.

No. 4 - No limousines, flashy cars, and so on, used on company business
No. 5 - Live within your means.

Have a good "financial image:

- Make money
- Save Money
- Pay your bills.
- Be a good citizen in your community.

No. 6 - No profit from selling anything to your people.

No. 7 - Have a good personal image.

- Don't let money or success change you. Remember where you came from. Always be a good person.

No. 8 - Have a great family life.

- Spend time with your family.
- Take care of your family.

No. 9 - Always be a positive, personal example.

People respond to the things you do and the way you live more than the things you say.

No. 10 - Always have the highest standards of honesty and integrity.

- Be honest and "above board" in everything you do.
- Discourage and "questionable" activity among your people ar around the office.

Reputation

"Everything you do builds your reputation, either in a positive way or a negative way. You must work to build a positive reputation in your community."
—Art Williams

In Business, YOUR REPUTATION IS EVERYTHING. You can't fool people for very long. If you do what is right, you might get by for one day or one week, or even for one year, but sooner or later they are going to smell you out.

We decided in 1977 that we would close our doors before we would prostitute our philosophy of "doing what's right" for the consumer and for our people.

We wanted to go out there and build a reputation of

being good people, honest people, sincere people and that is what we have done.

Everyone who is part of the A. L. Williams team has a responsibility to build the kind of reputation that is a credit to our company.

A.L. Williams Leaders "Do What's Right."

No. 1 - People don't respect a stranger or salesperson who calls them on the phone at home.

A.L. Williams leaders don't conduct their business by telephone. We're "people people" and we recruit and sell people "one-on-one," "eyeball-to-eyeball," across the kitchen table.

No. 2 - People don't respect someone taking them to a meeting without explaining what it is all about.

A.L. Williams leaders are not ashamed of our opportunity, they're proud of it. We don't have to "hoodwink" people into coming to our meetings: our opportunity is too great for that.

No. 3 - People don't respect a company that mails out postcards, flyers, mailers and so forth to every home.

A.L. Williams leaders don't recruit by "mass mailings." We recruit people face-to-face.

No. 4 - People don't respect a computer or telephone machine calling them at their home and respect even less the company responsible for this i!mpersonal tactic.

A.L. Williams leaders don't resort to cold, impersonal ways of approaching people.

We have an image and reputation to uphold.

No. 5 - People don't respect their friends using them as "guinea pigs."

A.L. Williams leaders want to share the opportunity for security and financial independence with their friends, but they never "use" or "trick" their friends in any way.

No. 6 - Good people in communities generally don't read ads in newspapers.

A.L. Williams leaders recruit from their new recruit's warm market. They don't need the "impersonal" approach of running ads in the newspaper.

No. 7 - People don't respect companies that have booths at carnivals, fairs, etc., with "non-related" gadgets as a "come on."

A.L. Williams people don't have to "play games" to attract others to the opportunity

If you're committed and sincere, you can sell the opportunity without fancy "gimmicks."

No. 8 - Good people don't respect "con men/women," promoters or people who are too slick.

A.L. Williams leaders are "real people." They never "oversell" our business or our opportunity. They're always honest and sincere.

No. 9 - People don't respect companies that intimidate them with quotas or threats.

A.L. Williams leaders allow people to advance at their own pace. They practice the principle of "pushing up people."

No. 10 - People are fed up with salespeople who use high pressure, fast-talking, hard-closing techniques.

A.L. Williams leaders never sell on a first visit to a client. They always practice the "three-step sales process."

No. 11 - People don't respect "mealymouths" and "fencesitters" that sell anything just for a profit.

A.L. Williams leaders sell 100% term insurance, all the time.

No. 12 - People don't respect salespeople who aren't committed to their company and their product.

A.L. Williams leaders sell what they believe in owning on their own lives.

At A.L. Williams, we're going to be real people. We're not going to change.

We're not going to pretend to be something we're not. We're going to be real, sincere, honest and "above-board."

A Company Within a Company

"When A.L. Williams was formed in 1977, I said that an RVP is supposed to build a company within a company. But every company must have great leadership. As an RVP, you are responsible for everything that happens in your company."
—Art Williams

No. 1 - A.L. Williams believes that leadership is everything.

The RVP is our leader.

No. 2 - The RVP has his own business.

There are no "junior" RVPs.

No. 3 - Each RVP reports only to the company and his NSD, not to his upline RVP or SVP.

The only exceptions are in the areas of compliance and quality of business. All RVPs are expected to operate as a team and a family. We want a spirit of cooperation and respect.

No. 4 - The RVP has no excuse for failure.

RVPs have freedom and everything else they need to win.

No. 5 - The only thing that can cause an RVP to fail is himself.

Prestige vs. Opportunity

"We believe prestige comes after you win."
—Art Williams

A.L. Williams believes in giving you A REAL OPPORTUNITY to be everything you want to be. Many companies promote PRESTIGE. They give you a big office, a fancy title, a country club membership- but no opportunity. We believe prestige comes AFTER you win. A person makes a position, a position does NOT make a person. We will give you a fabulous opportunity, but it's up to you to "make it big" or to be "average and ordinary."

No. 1 - We reward those who "do it" at A.L. Williams.

We are NOT interested in resumes, degrees, experience and talk. We want the people who have the "responsibility and desire" to "PROVE" themselves at A.L. Williams.

No. 2 - "Excuses don't count" in the big leagues.

The major difference between a winner and a loser is: THE WINNER WON'T QUIT. He will "Do It" and "Do It" until he wins. We want ONLY WINNERS on our RVP team.

RVP Responsibility

"You can never have true freedom unless you have responsibility."
—Art Williams

The RVP is TOTALLY RESPONSIBLE for EVERYTHING that happens in his region. An RVP CANNOT blame anyone else for any mistake or failure. If the RVP is a REAL LEADER, his people will succeed and he will succeed. The RVP is RESPONSIBLE to be successful in 5 MAJOR AREAS:

No. 1 - RVPs must be everything to everybody.

RVPs must take a TOTAL COMMITMENT to their people. RVPs must KNOW EVERYTHING that goes on in their region. RVPs must do the following as long as humanly possible:

- Field train EVERY PERSON in their region.
- Recruit EVERY PERSON in their region.

- Sell EVERY PERSON "the dream" and the opportunity.
- Teach EVERY PERSON how to be "a crusader."
- Run EVERY Meeting.
- Run EVERY Fast Start School.
- Build a personal relationship with EVERY PERSON.

No. 2 - RVPs must expect to win and expect their people to win.

February 10, 1977- OUR GOAL- "To help our families become FINANCIALLY INDEPENDENT."

- Look at everybody as a winner
- "Close" only counts in horseshoes- we want to win
- "Circle the wagons"
  It is a PRIVLEGE to play on our team.
  - Always sell the dream.
  - Always sell the dream.
  - Always sell the dream.

No. 3 - RVPs must build "a company within a company."

RVPs should not do secretarial work. Their time is worth $200/ hr. if they're doing the right things. RVPs must have the organization and structure of a company in order to have unlimited growth.

RVPs must ...

- Know what's going on - "face-to-face" inspection.
- Have Fast Start Schools.
- Have training classes.
- Have "Drill for Skill" sessions. (Example: "How to give a winning presentation.")
- Have recognition meetings, seminars, retreats and conventions.
- Have refresher classes every 60 to 90 days.
- Build and maintain a big base shop.
- Produce 7 to 10 first generation RVPs.

No. 4 - RVPs must have a system.

The A.L. Williams system is THE BEST SYSTEM and THE ONLY SYSTEM.

- You must have a reason for everything you do
- You must be consistent
- Your system must be based on 2 principles:
  - The Golden Rule - "Do unto others as you would have them do unto you."
  - Common sense
    (It is almost impossible for "smart people" to win.)

No. 5 - RVPs must be a winning example.

RVPs must LEAD BY EXAMPLE and ALWAYS DO IT FIRST. The team must see the RVP PERFORMING and SUCCEEDING in every area.

Example:

- Build a big base shop.
- Make money and save money.
- Be the hardest worker.
- Be the greatest crusader.
- Be the most excited.

Time is the Key

"You can solve half of the problems of this business just by spending time with your people."
—Art Williams

Spending time with your people is THE SINGLE GREATEST INVESTMENT you will ever make. NOTHING you can ever do will mean more to the long-range success of your business.

The BIGGEST PROBLEM in this business is TIME - taking time to "do things right," Managing time and making time work for you in your business.

There are TWO REASONS that people don't buy from you, come to work for you, or make it at A.L. Williams:

- They don't understand.
- They don't believe.

you solve both of these problems by SPENDING TIME WITH PEOPLE.

Both SELLING and RECRUITING depend on time;

I believe that if you spent enough time, there's no one in the world you couldn't sell or recruit.

You can't "quick sell" our product or our opportunity.

Let's discuss FIVE SPECIFIC AREAS where time can work for you; of course there are numerous other examples.

No. 1 - Presenting awards

- Never present an award by just calling the name and giving a handshake.
- Always take a few minutes to talk about the person. Tell about his success, his contribution, his sacrifice, his family, and so on.
- Make the person feel "special" and unique.

No. 2 - First interview

- The first interview should last a minimum of 30-60 minutes. This interview is "all important."
- You don't get a second chance to make a first

impression; your first impression is EVERYTHING.

- The first visit with a client is for education - we don't sell at the first interview - but the client makes up his mind about YOU at the first interview. He will buy (or not buy) based on his first impression of you.

Remember: People don't buy the company. They buy you!

No. 3 - Recruiting interview

- Recruiting interviews should last from 5 to 10 hours.

No. 4 - Recruiting process

- First interview with husband and wife across the kitchen table = 30 to 60 minutes
- Final recruiting interview and completing hiring papers = 30 to 60 minutes
- Field training and office training (licensing, etc.)

- Fast Start School
- Start building a personal relationship with the new recruit and family
  (Example: Invite the new recruit to your home, a picnic, a retreat, etc.)

No. 5 - Building a business

It takes 3 to 5 years to build a successful business.

Most people FAIL because they don't give themselves enough time to really build a strong business. Owning your own business isn't a two-month proposition - IT'S A LIFETIME PROPOSITION.

Remember: I believe it's impossible for anyone to fail at A.L. Williams if he is willing to invest the time and do what it takes.

Time with People = Success

Other areas where time is critical

No. 1 - Recognition

You can never give TOO MUCH recognition.

No. 2 - Training

You must build crusaders. The more you learn, the greater crusader you become.

No. 3 - Building Personal Relationships

Get to know your people's goals and learn about their families.

No. 4 - Selling the dream

Retreats, award programs, Fast Start Schools, RVP meetings, conventions, etc.

No. 5 - Partners

Get the spouses involved in your business.

Prospecting the A.L. Williams Way

"In A.L. Williams, you don't have to be an "expert" salesperson. We take people who have never been in sales before and train them to win."

—Art Williams

A.L. Williams was built for GREENIES - people who are scared to prospect, scared to sell, and scared to live on commissions, but people who WANT TO BE SOMEBODY.

A.L. Williams' "kind of people":
A.L. Williams believes in "greenies."

- People "locked out" of corporate America by education or background.
- People who've been taken advantage of by big companies, who didn't have status or come from a "privileged" background.
- People who have been put down by companies who believe in a false standard of what it takes to be successful.

Most companies believe in "privileged" people.

- College degrees
- Born on the right side of the tracks
- Born to wealth or privilege
- High IQ and college board scores

If you do have those characteristics ...

- You get the good jobs
- You get the business opportunities

If you don't have those characteristics ...

- You get the low-status, low-paying jobs
- You get "cut out" of business opportunities

I believe ...

- That there has never been a test, and there never will be a test, that can measure THE HEART of a man or woman.

I believe ...

- That everybody wants to be somebody
- That desire and will to win are more important than college degrees and family background
- That "inside" qualities like determination and perseverance are more important than "outside" qualities.

A.L. Williams builds with people, whoever they are, who want to be somebody and do something special with their lives.

- Everybody starts at the same place (on the bottom) and is promoted based on their own ability and activity.
- There's no discrimination of any kind - male, female, black, white, etc. - you advance based on performance.

At A.L. Williams, we don't care where you've been - just where you're going!

- People are our greatest asset!

A.L. Williams "qualifications"

- We don't want "salespeople."
- We don't want "fancy people."
- We don't want "prima donnas."
- We don't want "insurance types."

We do want ...

- Average, ordinary, good people on the outside, but who have "the heart of a champion."

Fundamentals of Prospecting

"There are no shortcuts to building something good and special."
—Art Williams

No. 1 - Two ways to prospect:

- Recruiting first and then selling the recruit if he needs and wants the product. (You cannot require recruits to buy)

OR

- Getting a client and then recruiting the client. (Both are effective and productive.)

No. 2 - Best market (Minimum- 4 points)

- Age 25 and up
- Married
- Children
- Employed with $40,000 income
- Own a home

No. 3 - Recruit the "Natural Market"

This is important. Theoretically, you can recruit one person with 25 referrals in his natural market and never have to prospect, cold call or talk to a stranger again:

Example:

1 Recruit=
25 Referrals (natural market)=
10-12 Policy Pick-ups=
8-10 Sales=

4-5 Recruits =
100 to 125 Referrals (new recruits' natural markets)=
40 -60 Policy Pick-ups=
32 to 50 Sales=

16-25 Recruits=
400-626 Referrals =
160-250 Policy Pick-ups=
128-200 Sales =

64-100 Recruits =
1600-2500 Referrals=
640-1000 Policy Pick-ups =
512-800 Sales=

No. 4 - Best prospects

- Always- REFERRALS. It is impossible to win long-range unless you learn how to get and use referrals.

No. 5 - Best referrals

- The new client's or recruit's natural market

No. 6 - Protect the referrals

- Don't let new unlicensed recruits talk to them

No. 7 - Where to recruit

- Always across the kitchen table with husband and wife present

---

No. 8 - How long is the recruiting process?

- Minimum of 5 to 10 HOURS

No. 9 - Steps for working with referrals

- Meet referrals face to face across the kitchen table with a new recruit present.
- Pick up policies with a commitment
- Close the referral's personal sale
- Recruit the referral
- Get the new recruit out field training FAST

- Get the new recruit and spouse to the next Fast Start School

Recruit's Natural Market

"The best way to help your new recruit build a business is through his natural market."
—Art Williams

No. 1 - Always face-to-face

- Never by phone or mail- only **EXCEPTION** is contacting referrals ...

No. 2 - Always in teams (2 people)

- Never sell alone.
- The new recruit's presence adds credibility.

No. 3 - Two kinds of referrals from new recruit's natural market

Divide referrals into two categories:

- Best friends
  - New recruit calls and makes appointment to take you over to the prospect's house.
  - Unlicensed recruits may not discuss insurance.
- Good 4 and 5 points
  - (Points: Age 25 and up, married, children, employed with income of $40,000, own home)
  - You and new recruit drop by to meet referral and set up an appointment.

No. 4 - Purpose of the Client Night

To reinforce the concept and opportunity and show the bigness of A.L. Williams. NEVER to introduce the concept. NEVER to close the sale.

No. 5 - How long do you spend at the first interview?

30 to 60 minutes - minimum

No. 6 - The sale is made or the recruit is locked up during the first interview

---

You close the sale at the second interview, but you actually make that sale based on how well you do on the first interview. (First impressions are everything!)

No. 7 - Everyone should use the Asset Management presentation

---

Everyone in your entire region must use the asset management presentation 100% of the time. It is THE ONLY PRESENTATION.

No. 8 - Order of importance for a recruiting interview

- Who is A.L. Williams and what have we done?
- The concept - we want crusaders.
- A.L. Williams was built for and by "greenies."
- Don't worry about prospecting, sales, etc.
- We teach you.
- You're never alone- we're with you.

- $250 training and licensing reimbursement- practically no risk
- Financial opportunity- part-time
- Long-range: full-time management potential
- How to get started and commitment

No. 9 - How many recruits is enough?

- You can never recruit too many of the right kind of people. RECRUIT, RECRUIT, RECRUIT!

No. 10 - Two objectives while field training

- New recruit teams from the leader while field training. (One hour field training is better than ten hours in the classroom.)
- The credibility of the new recruit with his or her referrals makes the warmest and most positive atmosphere you can create in the sales business

---

No. 11 - New recruit's immediate goal

- Complete the \$250 training and licensing reimbursement program.
- No risk if you complete the program as you are reimbursed before you ever try to sell.

No. 12 - Leader and/or RVPs immediate goal

- 6 sales and 3 recruits on referrals from each new recruit. (Share commissions after recruit completes training reimbursement program.)
- Minimum of 1 new recruit per week.
- Field train the recruit

Recruiting

"I can sum this business up in three words: recruit, recruit, recruit."
—Art Williams

Recruiting is the LIFEBLOOD of our business. If you stop recruiting, you die.

No. 1 - Recruiting tips

Recruit all the time

Look at everyone as a possible recruit and recruit everybody.

- The "NO. 1 RVP" is always the "NO. 1 Recruiter" ...
  - The No. 1 earners are the No. 1 recruiters.
  - The No. 1 's on the Leaders Bulletins are always the No. 1 recruiters.
- Always remember: At every level, you are only one or two good recruits away from a "new surge."
  - You solve every problem in our business with a new recruit.
- Recruiting is the "lifeblood" of our business.
  - You must keep the pipeline full of recruits.
- Keep 'em coming and going.
  - Nothing excites the "old" people like the excitement of a new recruit.
  - Nothing excites the team like promotions. You can never recruit too many good people or have too many promotions.

- Initial concept is presented at home.
  - You sell the PRODUCT at home.
  - You sell the OPPORTUNITY at home.

No. 2 - Steps to recruiting the A.L. Williams Way

- Prospect by selling the opportunity. People are turned off by insurance, but almost everyone needs extra income.
- We have the best part-time opportunity in America. You can make a great extra income doing a great service for people. There's practically NO RISK and people are "double-dumb" not to give it a try.
- The best prospects are a recruit's natural market. If you are recruiting in the right market, your new recruits should have a MINIMUM of 10-25 qualified prospects in their natural markets.
- Protect your new recruit's natural market. Don't let the new recruit talk to his natural market about our business.
- Our best salesperson must sell and our best recruiter must recruit. The RVP and top leaders

must not become administrators, office trainers or motivators and let the new leaders and newly licensed recruits do the recruiting and selling. (THE MOST IMPORTANT FUNCTION in A.L. Williams is what takes place across the kitchen table.)

- A.L. Williams believes in a team concept. You should rarely recruit or sell alone. Take a new recruit or rep with you.
- Invite your new recruits and their spouses to your next Fast Start School.
  - You recruit "one on one" and you use Fast Start Schools to show the "bigness" of A.L. Williams, and to reinforce the concept...
- Get off to a fast start. Have a new recruit out field training within 72 hours. The quicker you get your recruit field training, the greater the odds of the recruit staying with you and getting licensed and becoming successful.
- Recruit A.L. Williams-type people. Age 25 and up, married, children, employed with income of $40,000 and own a home.
- Goals for field training a new recruit
  - Eight to 10 PPUs and/ or CNAs
  - Six sales and three recruits, or until new recruit is prepared to field train others.

- Mandatory - MINIMUM of 3 field training sales must be observed.

- 90 + % of recruiting is being excited.
  - Always be excited
  - Always sell the dream

Our Recruiting Concept

"To build financial independence, you must recruit 'wide' and 'deep.'"

—Art Williams

No. 1 - Recruit 7 to 10 wide and 4 deep

- Wide
  - New recruits: Recruit 7 to 10 wide
  - Get wider with every promotion
  - Example: New district, recruit 3 to 5 wider
- Deep
  - Go deep until you find 1 great recruit

  - If you go 4 deep, you should find 1 great recruit
  - One great recruit deep solidifies leg

No. 2 - 90 + % of recruiting is being excited!

- Direct - A personal recruit or a 1st generation recruit
- Leg - A group that produces 5 to 7 sales a month consistently
- Goals:
  - District leader - 7 to 1 0 directs, 2 legs
  - Division leader - 1 0 to 15 directs, 3 legs
  - RVP - 15 to 25 directs, 5 legs

No. 3 - Manage activity

- Work 4 nights a week in the field - 2 presentations a night AND
- Blitz - when momentum slows

No. 4 - Remember:

- Until you cash flow $10,000 a month consistently, you earn your living in the field.
  - Overrides should be treated as a "bonus" and never used to live on.
  - Build and maintain a "big base shop."

Be Careful Recruiting Salespeople

"Build it right the first time."
—Art Williams

Recruiting Principle: "A.L. Williams was built by recruiting greenies."

Be careful of recruiting "traditional" salespeople.

No. 1 - Poor reputation

- Often aren't the good people in the community
- Think they know everything
- Want to short-cut the system

- Interested in making money instead of helping people

No. 2 - No warm market

- Usually have exhausted warm market
- Have used friends by selling them other products or "schemes" that didn't work out

Danger list:

- Former insurance agents
- People who are currently licensed
- Agents who sell casualty, disability, medical insurance etc.
- People involved in multi-level marketing
- People involved in any other kind of direct sales that would create an obvious temptation to get A.L. Williams representatives or clients involved

---

No. 3 - The standard should be set on the front end.

Some of the guidelines to help you manage these people properly are as follows:

- Don't ever hire them.
- If you do, manage them much more closely than you would a greenie. You should almost have a mistrust for them for six months or a year until they prove they are AS CAPABLE AS A GREENIE.
- Let them know that A.L. Williams really does not like to hire these kinds of people.

No. 4 - Transition period

If a manager insists on recruiting a person with this kind of background, it must be clearly understood that the company will be lenient to the point of allowing them a transition period in which to get out of any conflicting business totally and into A.L. Williams. This should be a rare exception, because the company frowns upon ever hiring these kinds of people. And misuse of A.L. Williams clients or sales force may result in termination. If this is OFFENSIVE or UNACEPTABLE in any way to the new recruit, the licensing process should be stopped immediately, ON THE FRONT END. DO NOT SEND THE LICENSING PAPERS TO A.L. WILLIAMS.

Personal Profile

"The A.L. Williams Personal Profile' is a great tool to tell if your people are in the right market."
—Art Williams

No. 1 - The "Personal Profile" is a way of qualifying prospects. It can also tell you a lot about potential recruits.

As the RVP, you must monitor to make sure your people are recruiting in A.L. Williams' target market (age 25 and up, married, children, own their own home, have an income of $40,000+).

There are times when one of your leaders may have a prospect who is not in the right market but who seems "perfect for this business."

Everyone thinks his "exception" to the A.L. Williams target market is "different" and deserves a chance. With the Personal Profile, you can tell if the exception is just that - an "exception," or if your leader might be recruiting in a bad market.

No. 2 - How to use the Personal Profile

You can use the Personal Profile at all times in your organization, but you should especially try to use it when you notice a big increase in recruiting.

The Personal Profile is based on a point system. As a rule, your recruiting prospects should achieve a MINIMUM OF 50 POINTS on the Personal Profile before you accept their hiring papers.

No. 3 - Steps for use:

- Rep gives card to recruiting prospect to fill out
- Rep submits hiring papers to you, RVP, along with Personal Profile

The Personal Profile can be a guide to help you control the quality of people you recruit in your organization.

Good persistency in our business is accomplished by doing all of the right things in the front-end, like hiring GOOD people and selling GOOD markets. You can't solve a quality of business problem when you are reading your persistency reports - by then it is TOO LATE!

You can never recruit too many GOOD PEOPLE!
Personal Profile Card
Categories:

- Age - Must be over 25
- Employment - Self Employed best
- Length of Employment - 5 years or more best
- Marriage - over 3 years best
- Dependents - 2 to 4 best
- Life Insurance - Over $50,000 best
- Actual Monthly Expenses - Over $2,000 best
- Net Worth - Over $60,000 best
- Education - College Graduate best
- Income - Over $40,000 best

The Sales Process

"At A.L. Williams, we do not believe in high pressure sales. We take a low key, educational approach. We do not allow people to sell on a first interview."
—Art Williams

The A.L. Williams 3-Step Sales Process

No. 1 - First interview objectives:

- No sale on the first interview
- Explain our concept
- Pick up policies
- Get commitment from client - leave Common Sense and other third-party material

No. 2 - Second interview objectives:

- Go over comparison and proposal
- Make the sale
- Prepare for the enemy agent

No. 3 - Third interview objectives:

- Deliver the policy
- Reinforce the concept
- Make the securities sale

Important note: Never let the client cancel his current policies until his MILICO policy is issued and accepted.

Keys to Selling the A.L. Williams Way

"We sell only what the consumer needs - not what makes the most money for our company."
—Art Williams

No. 1 - Keep it simple

All the confusion and complexity in our industry were designed to confuse the consumer so agents could sell the consumer high-cost, low-value products.

YOUR JOB is to help the consumer understand our concept and our product.

No. 2 - Always put your client first

Sell only to the client's need. Example: Young, single people with no family responsibilities don't need insurance; don't sell them life insurance, start a good investment program.

No. 3 - No separate policy on wife or children (one policy per family)

The average policy fee is $25 to $50. If a family has five policies, they could buy one policy and take the administrative cost ($25 x 4 = $100) and buy $100,000 of term at age 30.

No. 4 - No life insurance on children

Maximum, if the client insists, should be a burial policy. The purpose of life insurance is to replace the income of the breadwinner.

No. 5 - Never sell at meetings

The ONLY place a sale should ever take place is IN THE HOME, one-on-one, with both husband and wife.

No. 6 - You don't have to buy our product to come to work for A.L. Williams

Nevertheless, you should "practice what you preach" by making sure your family is protected. A new person should only buy our product if he/ she needs it and qualifies for it. But don't be a phoney like so many in our industry who own one thing but sell another.

No. 7- At A.L. Williams, you can't "sell yourself

If you desire to buy the MILICO product when you come on board with A.L. Williams, you must buy from another A.L. Williams representative.

Field Training

"Field training is the single most important area of activity in your business."
—Art Williams

You CANNOT SUCCEED unless you become an EXPERT in field training new recruits. 90% OF YOUR TIME SHOULD BE SPENT FIELD TRAINING!

No. 1 - How many field training sales should you make?

- You field train until the new recruit is prepared to field train others ...
- Minimum of 3 is required, but 6 is better ...
- Do whatever it takes ... 1 0, 15, more if necessary
  - Remember: the leader must make a total commitment first, before he can expect a commitment from the new recruit.

No. 2 - You must "lock-in" the new recruit!

The MORE policy pick-ups, sales and recruits you get while field training, the tougher it is for the new recruit to quit ... (split commissions after recruit is licensed and he can participate in sale.)

No. 3 - You field train "7 to 10 wide" and "4 deep"

- "Wide:"
  - New recruit should recruit 7 to 10 direct
  - At every level, keep getting wider ...
  - Example - New district leader recruits 3 to 5 direct
- "Deep:"
  - If you work 4 deep, you will recruit one outstanding prospect
  - One great recruit deep will solidify the leg

No. 4 - When is a sales leader prepared to field train?

- To qualify to become a sales leader, you must have:
  - 2 direct recruits
  - 6 personal sales
- Do 2 recruits and 6 sales automatically qualify a sales leader to field train?
  - No way!

No. 5 - What must a sales leader be able to do before field training a new recruit?

- Give a fantastic Asset Management presentation (only presentation to use)
- Destroy the competition
- Analyze policies and understand completely our ADS comparisons and proposals
- Be a good enough recruiter to get the prospect to the Client Night ...
- Know how to get referrals - 3 ways
  - — New recruit's referrals
  - — Referrals from clients
  - — FORM - turning strangers into friends
- Be capable of making a positive impression with the recruit and the prospect

---

No. 6 - When do you know the sales leader is ready to field train?

- RVP is "TOTALLY RESPONSIBLE" to see that his leaders perform ...
  - — It is not the responsibility of your management team to "train the trainers," it is
  - — YOUR responsibility.
- Be "TOUGH" on your leaders ...
  - — Must be crusaders

  - Must be good
  - Must win
- It is a PRIVILEGE to wear our uniform. You must be "double-tough" to be a leader on our team!
- RVP "PERSONALLY INSPECT" each new sales leader before allowing him to field train ...
  - In private interview
  - In training classes
  - Mandatory - observe Asset Management presentation

No. 7 - Make sure your entire organization understands that every person's No. 1 responsibility is to field train

---

- 90% of your time must be field training
- Most important function in A.L. Williams
- Mandatory that you are an excellent field trainer before you earn promotions
- You must be A COMPETITOR
  - Make every sale
  - Recruit every prospect
  - Be No. 1 on Leaders Bulletins
  - Knock out competition

No. 8 - Give yourself a chance to win: manage activity:

- Set "standard of excellence" for your field trainers:
  - 4 nights a week, 2 presentations a night
  - When your momentum slows, start a blitz
- Keep "a record" (update daily) of field training activity.
  - Field training presentations
  - Policy pick-ups
  - Sales
  - Recruits
- Create competition among your field trainers ...
  - Make your best field trainer a "hero"
  - Recognize and reward good field training activity

No. 9 - You (the RVP or the leader) be "the best" and "most active" field trainer.

- You set "the pace" for your team
- You be the hardest worker in the field

No. 10 - RVP must have "refresher courses" for field training!

- Check up and eliminate short cuts
- Stress fundamentals again (crusaders)
- Sell the Dream

No. 11 - If field trainer goes into "a slump," you immediately sell him the Dream again, recruit for him again and start the whole process again

---

Don't give up on your people. Believe in them and help them overcome the tough times.

No. 12 - Prepare your recruits for the "toughness" of A.L. Williams

---

- Let them know that this is a tough business. (We didn't get to be No. 1 in our industry by "taking it easy.")
- Let them know that, if they're going to play on your team, they've got to "play hurt."
  - Come to work every day
  - Get licensed
  - Get started field training.
  - Learn the business "inside and out"
  - Asset Management Presentation - the concept
  - Study and learn what A.L. Williams believes
  - Attend training classes
  - Attend A.L. Williams meetings
  - Encourage their spouses to participate and attend
  - Work, work, work!
- Let them know that it's OK to be scared.
  - We don't want "professional" salespeople.
  - We don't expect people to know the business ... we train them in everything they need to know.
  - Honesty and sincerity and "a burning desire" are the most important characteristics in a new recruit.
- Help people understand that they don't have to do it alone. The manager/RVP relieves the recruit's biggest fears:

- Fear of "not knowing" - YOU will train
- Fear of sales - YOU will talk to clients until they learn
- Fear of prospecting - YOU will recruit until they learn
- Fear of going out alone -YOU will field train "as long as it takes" for them to feel comfortable

But ...

- Recruits must understand that they've got to "tough it out" through the discomfort, the uneasiness and the fear if they want to make it.

Remember ...

People who want to be comfortable, who want to have it easy, can work at McDonalds. But they will never build FINANCIAL INDEPENDENCE and TOTAL SECURITY for their families by taking it easy.

No. 13 - The way to survive the "tough times" ...

You've got to be a "crusader." Develop a crusading attitude, believe in what you're doing and be willing to fight for what you believe is right. If you believe in what you're doing, you can survive whatever comes your way.

A Winning Presentation

"People buy you, as much as they buy a company or product."
—Art Williams

What is the difference between a $5,000 a year salesperson and a $100,000 a year salesperson? I believe it is THE WAY YOU FEEL ABOUT W'HA T YOU DO!

It is amazing how two people can get the same training, sell the same products, use the same presentation, have the same ability, and one person will be ultra-successful and the other will be average and ordinary!

Nowhere else in your business is "BEING A CRUSADER" more important than in giving a presentation - it determines success or failure.

As a leader in A.L. Williams, it is critical that you make sure your people can give a winning presentation.

"Two ways" to give a presentation

You and your people must "MASTER" 2 ways to "tell our story."

No. 1 - Asset Management Presentation

- Everyone uses the Asset Management presentation "exclusively."
- There is no way you can CONTROL AN ORGANIZATION unless everyone is doing the same presentation.

No. 2 - The "eye opener"

- This presentation is ONLY to be used when you're prospecting and you don't have your Asset Management flip chart OR you're trying to interest a prospect in a first interview; It must be followed by the Asset Management presentation when you get the interview with the prospect.

Remember: people remember 85% of WHAT THEY SEE and only 15% of WHAT THEY HEAR.

Explanation of "No. 1" Asset Management Presentation ...

- The "KEY" to the success of your business ... (Your presentation is everything)

- The first impression is critical... (People buy "you" as much as they do a company or product
- You must be able to give our presentation from FRONT TO BACK, BACK TO FRONT, and SIDEWAYS ... (You must know every word, every thought and every concept.)
- You must be FABULOUSLY EXCITED ... (90+% of winning is being excited.)

A few guidelines:

- The RVP is TOTALLY RESPONSIBLE for seeing that all of his people (especially field trainers) can give a GREAT presentation.
  - The RVP must personally observe all field trainers giving a presentation before they are allowed to field train.
  - The RVP must have training classes where he instructs personally on how to give a GREAT presentation.
  - The RVP must have refresher classes on the importance of the presentation
- Everyone uses The A.L. Williams Asset Management Presentation exclusively. There is no way you can control an organization unless everyone is doing the same presentation.

- The top priority of your training program must be how to give a great presentation.

Expect your people to be crusaders. Expect your people to be EXCITED and ENTHUSIASTIC. Expect your people to give a GREAT presentation.

Explanation of "No. 2." - the eye opener ....
This can be given to interest prospects in an interview. It's a quick way to "open their eyes" to the problems with cash value insurance and the difference in amount of protection between cash value insurance and term insurance.

Be sure to let clients know that you will explain the entire concept fully in your complete

Asset Management presentation.

Age 25

$50/mo. Cash Value Insurance

Age 25 - Protection - $53,000
Cash Value - $ 0

Age 65 - Protection - $53,000
Cash Value - $30,000

1) Poor Return- 1% - 3%
(average according to 1979 FTC Report)

2) Cost to borrow - average 6 - 8% or more
3) Lose if die

$50/mo. Buy Term & Invest Difference

Age 25 -	Protection	- $53,000
	Savings	- $0
Age 65 -	Protection	- $53,000
	Savings	- + 64,000

1) Good return - 7 - 8% or more
2) No cost to borrow (your $)
3) Savings + face amount if die

Age65

$50/ mo. - Cash Value vs. Term

Die -	C.V.. $53,000	- Term - $117,000
Savings	C.V. -30,000	- Term - 64,000

How to use the "eye opener"

- You can give the "eye opener" presentation anywhere - on a plane, in the line at the grocery store, at a restaurant. The purpose of the "eye opener" is to entice the client to want to know more. It should only take 5 or 10 minutes.

- First, show the client what his $50 might buy in a typical cash value life insurance policy
- Emphasize the generally poor rate of return on the cash value element of C.V policies, (according to the FTC report) AND the fact that you pay for both protection and cash values but you only get one.
- Now, compare what your someone might have by spending $50 on a term life insurance policy and separate accumulation program. Emphasize the same protection with more than TWICE the savings (non guaranteed). And, that you get BOTH.
- Last explain the Age 65 example. Show the client the difference in term and cash value insurance at age 65- $34,000 MORE savings (non guaranteed) and $64,000 MORE protection with "BUY TERM AND INVEST THE DIFFERENCE!"
- Once you've gotten your client's attention (and the "eye opener" is a sure way to do it!), make an immediate appointment to sit down with them and show them the complete Asset Management presentation.

THE "EYE OPENER" IS A SURE-FIRE "DOOR OPENER"!

Keys to Making A Winning Presentation

"First impressions are everything. Remember, people don't buy the company. They buy you."
—Art Williams

No. 1 - Be yourself

- We are plain talking, conservative, positive, excited, tough-minded people ... don't pretend to be something you aren't

No. 2 - Dress like the people you are talking to expect you to dress

- Field trainers - Coat and tie if the prospect doesn't know you. (If prospect doesn't have on tie, loosen tie)

- New recruits - If you are visiting a friend, don't look like a sales person. Dress casual

---

No. 3 - Create the right setting

- Be excited- 90+% of winning in every area of our business is being excited.
- Be friendly - Warm up the prospect. Make him comfortable. Talk about football, hunting, etc. for a few minutes.
- Be sincere and serious - When you start talking business, be dead serious. No jokes. etc. You are talking about a family's financial future.
- Don't over-promote or over-sell- You don't have to. One of your biggest problems is that your prospect will feel our concept is "TOO GOOD TO BE TRUE." We are right, so tell it like it is.
- Keep it simple - Our competition has complicated a simple business so as to confuse the consumer. We help make it simple again.
- Put the prospect at ease- We don't sell on the first interview.

- We don't just sell policies- If we can't save you money (and I mean big money), we don't deserve your business.
- Sell A.L. Williams and MILICO - No. 1 (National Champions) in term insurance and individual insurance ... $65.5 billion in 1985 ... beat Prudential... 100,000 +people.
- When you receive an "objection" always "agree and go on with" your presentation ... You answer: "I understand why you feel that, I used to think the same way, but look what I found out!"
- Let the client know A.L. Williams isn't the typical insurance company and you aren't the typical salesman. If you don't like typical insurance people, you will like A.L. Williams.
- Expect the prospect to be cool, questioning and skeptical at first. You are not an ORDER TAKER You are a salesperson. Your job is to turn a prospect into a happy client.
- Don't be a "phony." Make sure your own program is an example of what everyone should own personally, i.e., not whole life!
- Pick up the policies. Don't leave without the policies. There is NO CHARGE for us to analyze their program and they would be foolish not to let us

compare our program with theirs and see if we can save them big money.

- Get a commitment. Find out if they are IN LOVE with their insurance agent. That is about the only time a prospect doesn't do business with A.L. Williams. (And by the way, not many people are in love with their insurance agent.)

After you pick up policies with a commitment, talk about "the Opportunity."

Isn't this unbelievable ...

— Do you know anybody who would like to save money?
— A.L. Williams- Greatest part-time opportunity in America
— Pay only license fee
— $250 training and reimbursement program (practically no risk)
— Something you feel good about - Ain't like selling soap, shoe polish, vitamins, diet drinks ...
— You don't need to know anything but this: what we do is "RIGHT FOR PEOPLE."
— We teach you and work with you- You're NEVER ALONE

— How could you use extra income each month?

- Get the recruits to the next Fast Start School. The purpose of the Fast Start School is to reinforce the concept and to show the bigness of A.L. Williams
- Have "good third party material" to leave with prospects while you analyze their policies
  — Common Sense, Saturday Evening Post, reprint, FTC Report, and so on.

Referrals

"You can't win in A.L. Williams or in the sales business unless you master the art of getting and working referrals."
—Art Williams

A.L. Williams has 3 basic referral systems:

No. 1 - New recruit's natural market

By FAR the BEST. 90% of your sales and recruits should come from this system.

Step 1. Sell the opportunity.

- Everyone needs extra income
- Greatest extra income opportunity in America

Step 2. Recruit the natural market.

- New recruit's personal sale is the least important thing.
- Don't let the new unlicensed recruit talk to his natural market.
- If you become an expert in working referrals, you will never have to prospect, cold call or talk to a stranger.

Step 3. Referral letters signed by recruits.

- Qualify each referral into 2 groups
- Best friends
- 4 and 5 pointers (DO NOT mail letters- keep in file to use if you are unable to contact referral in person)

Step 4. Two ways to contact the natural market

- Best friends - New recruit calls his best friend and sets up an appointment

— 4 and 5 pointers - New recruit and leader use "go by system" to introduce leader to his natural market and set up appointments for later date ....
— If you don't have a scheduled appointment later, and if the prospect has time - go ahead and have a full first interview ....

Step 5. Remember- Field train "7 to 10 wide" and "4 deep"
— The more policy pick-ups and recruits you get, the more you LOCK IN the new recruit.

No. 2 - "Friends" of a happy client

You should recruit a minimum of 25% to a maximum of 50% of your clients. Friends of a happy client are great prospects.

Steps to getting friends as referrals

Get "10 referral letters" signed

Qualify referrals (4 and 5 pointers) and find out as much as possible about the referrals.

How do you ask for referrals?

Prepare a summary - for example:

Age 65

1) Die - old $100,000 new - $213,000
2) cash - old $45,000 new - 183,000
3) cost - old $40/mo. new - $40/mo.

Step 1 -Resell the summary; make client FEEL GOOD again

Step 2 - Questions

— Do you understand?
— Do you feel good?
— Do you have any questions?

Step 3 - Name, would you be EMBARRASSED to recommend my service to your closest friends if I could do the same for them?

How do you contact the referral?

Step 1. Mail the referral letters
Step 2. Call the prospect on the phone

Things to say to the referral on the phone

Name, this is ________ of A.L. Williams. I recently sent you a letter, did you receive it?

The purpose of my call is to schedule an appointment to see if you, like (name), have need of our services.

In fact, you might want to call -------

I will be in your area next _______ , would 7 or 9 be better?

Referral Letter

Use this letter "as is" for best results ...

Date ________________________

Dear ________________________

Every so often, an opportunity comes along that can help us, but in our daily rush to keep things rolling, we ignore it.

I had the pleasure recently of being referred by a friend to review a program that is important to me financially, especially in these difficult times.

When I was first approached, I had little interest in even talking about it. But, because it is worthwhile and important, I recommend that you take the opportunity to hear about this program, also.

I asked _____________________ (name of A.L. Williams rep) to contact you in the near future. Make up your own mind, naturally, but it is my sincere belief you will find the short time it takes to be time well spent.

Sincerely,
(the client)

No. 3 - Prospecting with the "form" method.

Objectives: Warm up a cold market by turning strangers into friends.

Step 1. How it works:

It's simple. When you meet someone new, talk to him or her about the FOUR THINGS THAT APPLY TO EVERYONE:

— Family
— Occupation
— Recreation
— Money

Step 2. Two advantages to the form method:

- It's great for "breaking the ice" and getting to know people AND
- It's great for "qualifying" people while you talk to them.

For example:

— Recruiter: "Do you have a family, Joe?"
— Prospect: "yes, I have two boys and one girl?"

THAT TELLS YOU: The prospect fits into the qualifying category, because he's married with a family and obviously older than 25.

or

— Recruiter: "Do you have a family, Joe?"
— Prospect: "No, I'm not married."

THAT TELLS YOU: To be cautious. This person has few responsibilities and may not be interested in extra income or a part-time opportunity.

Step 3. Using the "friendship" concept

- The idea behind the form method is meeting new people and making new friends.
- The best part about this method of recruiting is that it's natural. Instead of going around cold calling, you recruit by building friendships with the people you meet every day. It's the idea of RECRUITING AS A LIFESTYLE.
- It's easy, and it's enjoyable.

- RECRUIT 24 HOURS A DAY, WHEREVER YOU ARE.
  - Recruit where you do business
  - At the supermarket
  - At the clothing store
  - At the dry cleaners
  - With service people (plumbers, etc.)
- GET TO KNOW PEOPLE AS INDIVDUALS. (NSD Larry Weidel says, "If you've made a friend in the last five years, or in the last year, or if you've EVER made a friend ... THEN YOU KNOW HOW TO PROSPECT!")
- REALLY BE INTERESTED IN PEOPLE. You'll make more friends in an afternoon by being interested in other people than you'll make in a year trying to get people interested in you.

The secret:

— Eye contact
— Shake hands
— Talk one-on-one
— Be sincere

The method:

Introduce yourself to someone you meet in the grocery store, hardware store, etc. ("By the way, my name's John Smith.") Whenever you're in the neighborhood, stop by and say hello. Talk about what he's interested in and just get to know him.

Build your relationship as a friend. (Whether the person is ever interested in our company or not, you can't have too many friends.)

Once you get to know the person on a FIRST NAME BASIS, talk to him about your business. (Very likely, he'll ask you about what you do for a living FIRST. Then you can take that opportunity to explain the company to him.)

- BE ALERT TO WHAT'S GOING ON AROUND YOU.

Example: You see a department store manager handle a difficult situation well. You think he'd make a good recruit. Go over and introduce yourself and tell him so. ("You certainly handled that situation well. You seem to have a real touch with people. By the way, my name's John Smith."- You've started to build a new friend!)

Other Ways to Prospect

No. 1 - Hand out Common Sense

- Many A.L. Williams representatives have found that Common Sense is a great way to introduce a potential recruit to a "common sense" financial philosophy.
- It's simple to show people with Common Sense.
- Here's how:

Step 1 - Work in teams (two people).
Step 2 - Each week hand out 10 copies of Common Sense (five each person).
Step 3 - Commit to this plan for one month.

Step 4 - Follow up one week later and talk about the book and the opportunity, "one-on-one."

No. 2 - Keep a client list

- Keep a list of all your clients.
- If you hit a "dry spell," go back to your clients ...
- RECRUIT YOUR CLIENTS. Timing is everything. The client who wasn't interested 6 months ago might be interested today.
- GET MORE REFERRALS. Satisfied clients give the best referrals. Your client will have new friends and acquaintances that he could suggest for our program. ·
- SERVICE YOUR CLIENTS. The family may need some adjustment or additional coverage to their policy. Your clients appreciate your "checking in" from time to time. Creates a good image for you and A.L. Williams.

No. 3 - Lunchtime prospecting

- A good way to encourage activity to a new rep who's having trouble getting started or an "old-timer" who's in a slump.
- Call the recruit or oldtimer and tell him you're treating him to lunch on a specific day that week.
- Ask him to bring one or two people with him who might be interested in the opportunity.
- You take charge and talk to the prospect(s); you sell the dream and the opportunity.
- You pay for the lunch - makes you more serious and makes you see the time as "more valuable."
- Follow up a few days later with the prospect by phone. ("John, I sure enjoyed meeting you at lunch Tuesday. I look forward to seeing you at our Opportunity Meeting next week.")

Note: Some managers go to lunch TWICE A DAY, at 11:00 and 1:00. This amounts to 2-4 recruiting interviews a day.

No. 4 - Centers of influence

- Many people have had success with this "indirect" approach.

Method: Approach people who are respected and influential in the neighborhood or community and ask for referrals.

Example:

"I'm new in this area and I need your help. My company has a great business opportunity to offer. We need honest, hard-working people to train for management positions. How can I go about finding that kind of person? Who do you know that I could talk to that might be good?"

- Good contacts:
  - Other independent business owners. (You have a "common bond.")
  - MINISTERS. (They know the good, honest people in the community.)
  - YOUR PARTNER. (One of the most overlooked areas. Your partner meets people every day!)
  - PEOPLE IN "LIKE OCCUPATIONS." (If you're a former coach, talk to other coaches, etc.)

No. 5 - Pick up business cards and/ or names

- Teach your people to ALWAYS LOOK for good prospects- especially when they're shopping. Pick up business cards and/ or names of the salespeople who help you.
- Everywhere you go - shopping, to a ballgame, to play golf, to a meeting, etc. -look for a prospect and get names and phone numbers!
- Take business cards and/ or names with phone numbers to your RVP or leader.
- RVP or leader calls the prospect for you and sets up an appointment during the day for breakfast, lunch, after work, etc.
- Face-to-face or phone contact- 'You don't know me by name, but one of our reps was in your store a few days ago and told me that you were a super salesperson (or whatever). [NAME] said you would be great in our business. We have a fabulous part-time opportunity and also great management positions. I'm just calling to see if you have a few minutes sometime during the day when we could visit."

Base Shop Guidelines

"It is impossible for an RVP to build successful RVPs and not maintain a strong base shop."
—Art Williams

The base shop is **"the key"** to an RVP being successful in A.L. Williams.

There is no other area as critical to your long-range success.

Why build a strong base shop?

No. 1 - You must "prove" that you can "win" at A.L. Williams before your people will "believe in" and "follow" you ...

- The only way to compete on the Leaders Bulletins and the income reports is to build a big base shop ...
  (People won't bet their business life on a DUD.)

No. 2 - It is your "source of income" until you build a big, strong RVP team.

- You should never count on overrides until you consistently cash flow $10,000 each month (you must personally make a living for your family).
- It takes a minimum of 25 RVP overrides to equal base shop override.
- You cannot rely on the income from your RVPs until you have 7 to 10 first generation RVPs.
- Your base shop is just like personally producing as a district leader.

No. 3 - You will not "lose touch" with your people ...

- You will be with your people daily. You will know immediately the income, the attitudes, activity and problems of your people.

No. 4 - It is the "best place" to build "personal relationships."

- It is the only way you can get to know your people and let them get to know you. Living with your people is the only way you can build the tremendous LOYALTY and the SPECIAL PERSONAL RELATIONSHIPS that will cause your people to believe in you and trust you as a leader.

No. 5 - You will not "lose" your "mental toughness" ...

- It is tough to run a base shop. You must continue to do the fundamentals. You are fighting every day.
- You will NEVER "lose the skills" that "make the difference" in "winning and losing."

No. 6 - You can be "the example" for your people ...

- By running a successful base shop, you take all the excuses away from your RVP.
- When your RVP says ... YOU can say ...
  — "Nobody's recruiting ... " (MY base shop is.)
  — "Nobody's sellmg .... " (MY base shop is.)
  — "I'm not making any money ... " (I am.)
  — "I can't run a base shop and work with RVPs too ... " (I do.)

No. 7 - The base shop is "where the action is."

- The activity in A.L. Williams begins and ends in the base shop.
- Something should be happening all the time. If the leader is there, he or she can help create the mental attitude that is necessary to keep people coming and going, and keep people "up" and positive. If the leader is at the office every day, he can help control activity and attitudes.

No. 8 - A successful base shop demands a "positive attitude."

- If the attitude and atmosphere of your base shop is right, your activity and your people's activity will be right.
- You must be excited, positive, and have the right attitude; and you must make sure your people have that attitude, too. If you maintain a positive attitude, you will be successful and happy in all areas of your life.
- When do you "reduce" or "close down" your base shop?
  - Certainly not before you have 7 to 10 first generation lifetime RVPs (remember an RVP should be earning a minimum of $80,000 a year and be an RVP for three to four years before you consider him a lifetime RVP ....
- Another rule of thumb would be - when you think you can no longer handle a base shop and do everything else you are supposed to do - wait two years ...
- How many "legs" should you have in your base shop "direct" to you?

  (Remember: a leg is 5 to 7 sales per month.)
  - To make a "good" living .. .5 legs
  - To make a "great" living ... 10 legs
  - To go "big-big time" ... 20 legs

No. 9 - There is a "danger" in relocating your base shop ...

- Moving your base shop to a new area can set you back a minimum of 2 years.

No. 10 - First generation RVP promotion "goals" from your base shop ...

- Financial independence - produce 7 to 10 1st Generation RVPs
  - Qualify for NSD - produce 15 to 20 1st Generation RVPs (plus complete other qualifications)
  - "All-time-great" in A.L. Williams- produce 20 to 25 1st Generation RVPs

Base Shop "Standard of Excellence"

Poor

Sales - 15 and below
Average Face Value - $99,000 and below

"So-So"

Sales - 16-29
Average Face Value - $100,000- $139,000

Good

Sales - 31-29
Average Face Value - $140,000- $199,000

Excellent

Sales - 50 and above
Average Face Value - $200,000 and above
*per month Sales

- Part-time: MINIMUM of 1 insurance sale per 6-month period
- SVP and below: MINIMUM 3 insurance sales each month in the base shop

- To qualify for RVP: MINIMUM $30,000 submitted annualized premium in one month after promotion to Regional Manager, have securities license and acceptable persistency.
- Savings goal - Total financial independence
  - Part-timers - Save and invest total part-timer income
  - Full-timers - Save and invest 50% of cash flow
- Business expense goal - Be lean and mean RVPs - spend a maximum of 20% (ideally 15%) of total cash flow for all business expenses. (Regional Manager and below pay no rent, fees, etc.)

150-Mile Rule

"Building leaders at home, helping them grow to be strong and successful, and then sending them out to 'conquer the world' is the A.L. Williams Way to build a successful business."

—Art Williams

It is absolutely critical that you understand your responsibility is "to deliver for your people." You CANNOT recruit people at a GREAT DISTANCE and manage them properly.

No. 1 - You build a successful business like you build a successful family.

A CHILD comes into the world scared and dependent.

A GREENIE comes into the world scared and dependent.

You must have a home with "LOVE AND WARMTH" so the child can grow to be strong and prepared, and so he can feel good about himself and challenged to "MEET AND SUCCEED" in the opportunities of the adult world.

The 150-Mile "Rules":

- "RVPs only" can recruit over 150-miles from their base shop ...
- "No replacement" taken from any recruit over 150-miles ...
- RVP can have only 1 base shop ... If you take on a rep who lives more than 150 miles from your

office, he would be entitled to an automatic transfer to a closer RVP.

150-Mile "Guidelines":

- NO ONE (including an RVP) should ever recruit over 150-miles ...
- Regional Managers and below should not recruit anyone OVER 50-MILES ...
- If a part-timer RELOCATES OVER 150-MILES because of his full-time job, you should REASSIGN HIM to a LOCAL RVP.
- If you or one of your people knows a good prospect over 150-miles give this REFERRAL to a local RVP.
- If you ever GIVE a referral away or TRANSFER any person, you CANNOT receive any compensation (replacement, etc.) of any kind in the future ...

Opening an Office

"RVPs must have an office and a secretary before they can build a great business. But they have a responsibility to have the kind of office that is a positive reflection of A.L. Williams."
—Art Williams

All RVPs should have a goal of opening their own office. It's an important part of the own your own business" concept that's a critical part of the A.L. Williams way.

But, they must always remember that any A.L. Williams office is a reflection of the company as a whole. Just like any franchise business or business "chain" must set certain "STANDARDS" for their managers, our company must also ask that our leaders keep certain guidelines in mind when they open a new office.

We must always be sure that A.L. Williams offices present an image of STABILITY and DECENCY to the community in which they're located.

No. 1 - RVPs must have an office OUTSIDE THEIR HOME and a secretary or answering service.
No. 2 - RVPs only can open an A.L. Williams office and must have the approval of their NSD.

Guidelines for opening an office

No. 1 - NSDs must approve new offices opened by RVPs (review lease, examine facility to approve design and budget).
No. 2 - Remember image and reputation.

- When an RVP opens an office and puts the A.L. Williams name on the door, he/ she has a responsibility to maintain the image of A.L. Williams.
  - Office should be in a good neighborhood
  - Office should look professional - not "fancy," but clean and well-kept
  - Office should be a reasonable size and arranged to fit the functions of an A.L. Williams office.
  - Office should be "stable" - don't want offices opening and closing all the time

— Note: No person below the RVP level can open an A.L. Williams office.

No. 3 - Only financially successful and financially strong RVPs may open an office.

- The NSD must approve the opening of a new RVP office.
- You must have a CASH FLOW of a MINIMUM of $8,000 - $10,000 a month for three consecutive months.
- You must have an EMERGENCY FUND with a MINIMUM of $20,000.
- You must have produced 1-2 RVPs.

No. 4 - Regional Managers and below pay no office expenses or fees.

No. 5 - If the NSD does not approve an RVP opening a new office, the RVP should cluster.

No. 6 - If you don't wish to cluster with your upline RVP, you may cluster with someone outside your hierarchy, with the special permission of your NSD.
No. 7 - RVPs should have a goal of paying a maximum of 15% of their cash flow to total business expenses.

- Every RVP who is financially ready should have an office and a secretary.
- Offices should be clean, attractive and functional - NOT big, showy and expensive.
  (Remember: You make money in the field, not in the office!)
- Expenses such as rent, telephone, equipment, etc. should be under the name of the RVP and NOT under the name of A.L. Williams.

No. 8 - RVPs should be cautious when considering expansion.

- Never expand your office until three months AFTER you think its necessary.
  — Don't "jump the gun" just because things are going good. Remember that you get charge-backs, people leave and so on, but you are committed to pay your rent. Give yourself an extra three months to make sure your success is "for real."

Clustering

"Custering is TEMPORARY, only until new RVPs get "on their feet" and are making enough money to have an office of their own."
—Art Williams

Important "clustering" guidelines:

No. 1 - When a leasing RVP agrees to allow new RVPs to "cluster," he/she must write the appropriate NSD a letter OUTLINING THE DETAILS OF THE CLUSTERING AGREEMENT THEY HAVE MADE.

This agreement should be signed by both the clustering RVP and the leasing RVP.

The letter should list total office expenses, number of clustering RVPs, how much the leasing RVP will pay, and how much the clustering RVP will pay.

The office should be in the name of the leasing RVP (lease, utilities, etc.).

No. 2 - In an A.L. Williams office, the leasing RVP ONLY should have a private office.

One private conference office should be provided for use by the clustering RVPs, Regional Managers and leaders to give recruiting interviews or conduct training meetings when.necessary, but they SHOULD NOT HAVE PRIVATE OFFICES.

The only private office a clustering RVP can have is AT HOME.

No. 3 - The only phone with a LONG DISTANCE LINE should be the phone in the leasing RVP's office.

Phones at secretary's desk and "bullpen" should be for LOCAL CALLS ONLY.

No. 4 - Each office should have a 'War Room" for client night.

Folding tables and chairs should be provided so the room can be used as a daytime work area.

No. 5 - Each clustering RVP will be assigned the use of the War Room for meetings.
No. 6 - Clustering RVPs pay their FAIR SHARE of office expenses.

What is a "fair share" will be established between the leasing RVP and clustering RVP and stated in the letter sent to the NSD for approval.

Clustering RVPs MUST PAY THEIR OFFICE EXPENSES DUE THE RVP. The promoting RVP should never be put in the position of "bill collector."

If a clustering RVP does not pay the "fair share" for ANY CONSECUTIVE THREE MONTH PERIOD, the promoting RVP should report this in writing to his NSD.

IF THE NSD CONFIRMS THAT TIME IS TRUE, THE CLUSTERING RVP WILL BE DEMOTED TO REGIONAL MANAGER.

(EXAMPLE: If the clustering RVP has agreed to pay $300 a month in January, and does not pay it in January or February, he is $600 behind. If he does not pay the full $900 in March, he may be demoted to Regional Manager by the NSD.)

If a clustering RVP is demoted to Regional Manager for lack of paying bills, he/ she MUST WAIT SIX MONTHS and MAKE UP THE DEBT BEFORE BEING ALLOWED TO REQUALIFY FOR THE RVP POSITION.

No. 7 - RVPs should not cluster with MORE THAN 4 OR 5 NEW RVPS. This gives each one night for necessary meetings.

No. 8 - An RVP cannot force another RVP to cluster.

Super Clustering

Two or three strong RVPs who qualify to have their own offices may house together with their clustering RVPs) in a large office space.

- In the "super clustering" situation, BOTH RVPS should sign the lease; BOTH SHOULD HAVE A SECRETARY and a PRN ATE OFFICE.
- They should conduct their business as two separate offices with TWO WAR ROOMS, TWO PRNATE CONFERENCE ROOMS, etc.

Important: RVP entering a super clustering situation should be COMPATIBLE, LONGTIME FRIENDS, STRONG EARNERS in stable financial condition and have a STRONG DESIRE AND COMMITMENT to make the arrangement work well.

"Ideal" RVP Office Setting

This office should be ideal for ONE RVP'S BASE SHOP.

You can cluster UP TO FOUR RVPS without increasing your office space. Clustering RVPs have access one night a week to the War Room for their meetings and do not need a private office, so they require no additional space. Clustering RVPs should be "coming and going" so, as you add new clustering RVPs, other will leave and you should not need to add space.

As you increase the number of"clustering" RVPs, you might need to ADD SECRETARIAL HELP. This is much CHEAPER than adding more space.

Goal: Keep clustering RVPs' expenses to a minimum so they can save money. (Goal for clustering RVP expenses: $600.00)

As the leasing RVP's income GOES UP, and as he promotes more clustering RVPs, expenses should GO DOWN. That will INCREASE AVAILABLE MONEY FOR SAVINGS and HELP DECREASE BUSINESS EXPENSES toward the goal of 15% for total business expenses.

Office Plan

No. 1. RECEPTION AREA

For secretary, waiting area for appointments, general "processing" area. If large enough, can be used for extra meeting area, if necessary.

No. 2. RVP OFFICE

Only "private" office

Remember: Long-distance phone line in RVP office ONLY; secretarial and "bullpen" phones should be LOCAL CALLS ONLY.

No. 3. WAR ROOM

For holding meetings. Folding tables and chairs should be available for daytime use as a workroom.

No. 4. PRIVATE CONFERENCE ROOM

Private office for recruiting interviews and training classes. Folding tables and chairs should be available.

NOTE:

1. Most office parks provide "outside" bathrooms, so that is not a consideration.
2. Many office parks have conference rooms you can use for additional meeting space, if needed.

Total office space:

1. MAXIMUM 950 SQ. Ff. (can be less)
2. PART-TIME SECRETARY OR ANSWERING SERVICE NO MORE THAN ONE YEAR LEASE, IF POSSIBLE

A.L. Williams Meetings

"Make your meetings count for something."
—Art Williams

Too many meetings are a complete waste of time. Always remember that you make Money "in the field - across the kitchen table."

Don't have a meeting just to have a meeting. Have a definite purpose for a meeting. You be prepared to make the meeting worthwhile for your people.

A great meeting can motivate your people like nothing else. A great meeting can Create FANTASTIC momentum.

I believe an RVP must master and perfect 6 kinds of meetings: Six kinds of meetings every RVP must perfect

---

No. 1 - Emergency meetings

Always the best meetings. Generate GREAT EXCITEMENT and TREMENDOUS anticipation.

No. 2 - Fast Start Schools

A career changing event, where new recruit and spouse make lifetime commitments (full and part-time) to A.L. Williams.

No. 3 - Manager (full-timers) meetings

Manager meetings should be used to CHECK ACTVITY (presentations, PPUs and recruits) and for TRAINING and MOTIVATION.

No. 4 - Training sessions

Use these sessions for building crusaders and "GETTING A MAD ON" at the competition.

No. 5 - Conventions and retreats

The "ULTIMATE" way to sell "THE DREAM."

Fundamentals:

RVPs or above are responsible for the format and conduct of all meetings held in their region. They work with other RVPs in inter-regional meetings.

- Different meetings have different purposes, but all meetings should comply with certain guidelines.
- Meetings should always be conducted by A.L. Williams people. No outside speakers should be used.
- Conduct the meeting in a professional manner - in conduct, dress and speech.
- Use the meeting as a way to recognize your leading producers and prospective RVPs.
- Allow the leaders to share their positive experiences with the group - never allow the meeting to become a complaint session.
- Never sell any materials other than A.L. Williams material. Even then, A.L. Williams material should be sold only as a convenience and at the price listed by the A.L. Williams Distribution Center.
- Charge a fee for a meeting only if it is necessary to cover expenses, but keep expenses to a minimum. Profit should never be made from meetings.

- Speakers should never charge a fee to speak and should be able to recoup only actual expenses.
- Use only approved sales, promotional and training materials.
- Present only the facts - never exaggerations. The A.L. Williams Opportunity is real and doesn't need exaggerations.
- Always end the meeting on a positive note.

Fast Start Schools

Purpose:

- To build crusaders
- To sell the Dream
- To train your people
- To put our GREAT LEADERS in an area in front of our people
- To help develop LEADERS into GREAT motivators and GREAT speakers
- To cross-pollinate organizations so the new recruits can learn from other teams

- A GREAT place for promotions. Very special recognition for those getting promoted and proves to everyone the Opportunity is for real.

Invite

Husband and wife to the Fast Start School. (This is a career-changing event.) Lifetime commitments (part-time and full-time) are made.

Also ...

The Fast Start School is a place where old-timers (part and full-time) can come together every six weeks to get remotivated, recommitted, and to be together as a team (like a family reunion or class reunion).

How often:

- Every six weeks

How long

The perfect length - Friday, 7:00 - 10:00 p.m.
Saturday, 8:00 - 5:00 p.m.
Sunday, 8:00 - 12:00 p.m.

Who (speakers) - Your best leaders ...

- First, by income
- Second, by production
- Third, by recruiting

- You want only those who "DO IT" to speak to your people!

Rules:

The atmosphere should be electrifying. Everything positive, fast, GO-GO-GO ...

- Keep track of time. Give speakers a time (usually 20 minutes) and stay on schedule ... have a large number of short parts, 2 and 5 minute ideas.
- Have good handouts. (Only those approved by A.L. Williams.)
- If you have enough room, use tables and chairs ... if not, spread out chairs as much as possible. Make it comfortable.
- Make sure the platform is high so that everyone can see.
- Check the sound and air conditioning in advance.
- No smoking, no alcohol, and no profanity.
- Never, EVER use any outside speakers.
- Never talk about anything but A.L. Williams.
- Make sure speakers cover their topics. Don't have everyone give his personal story and testimony.
- Try not to charge a fee, but if you must, keep it low ... $1, $2, etc., and never more than you need to cover costs.

- Never sell anything to the A.L. Williams people at any meeting or school.
- Never have drawings or give-aways.

A.L. Williams "First" Fast Start School
Friday - 6:30 - 9:30 p.m.*
Minutes - Speaker - Topic

5 - RVP - Welcome
20 - Art Williams - Why "Our" Company
20 - RVP - Decreasing Responsibility theory
20 - RVP - Asset Management presentation
20 - RVP - The Dream
break
20 - RVP - Mutual Funds
30 - Division Leader - Opportunity, Goals
10 - Art Williams - ALW's needs

Saturday - 7:30 a.m. - 5:00 p.m.
Minutes - Speaker - Topic

10 - Division Leader - Selling yourself and scheduling
30 - Art Williams - My personal story

---

* Recommend promotions the first night

15 - RVP - Policy pick-up and commitment
15 - RVP - Eye opener presentation
10 - Art Williams - Third party
break
15 - Regional Manager - Eye opener presentation
15 - Small group - Eye opener presentation
10 - District Leader - "3 Nevers" of buying insurance
10 - Art Williams - Is it legal?
5 - District Leader - Policy loans
10 - District Leader - Preparing for conserving agent
35 - Art Williams - Mental preparation
lunch
10 - 2 Division Leaders - Pillow fund
10 - District Leader - Mortality tables
5 - District Leader - Eye opener presentation
10 - RVP - Formula for $50,000 income
20 - RVP - Fundamentals
15 - Art Williams - How to sell "our" company
15 - Regional Manager - Referrals
15 - Division Leader - How to overcome objections
20 - RVP - Fundamentals
5 - Division Leader - Cost per 1,000
15 - RVP - Dividends

break
lo - Art Williams - Your responsibility
20 - District Leader - Asset Management presentation
10 - Small group - Asset Management presentation
5 - RVP - Eye opener
15 - RVP - 3 types of term
40 - Art Williams - Annuities and guarantees

Sunday - 8:00 a.m. - 12:00 p.m.

45 - Art Williams - Test
60 - RVP - Prospecting
20 - Regional Manager - Goal setting
10 - District Leader - Our business
break
20 - Small group - Asset Management presentation
15 - District Leader - Fundamentals
15 - RVP - Immediate goals
20 - Art Williams - Personal goal and commitment

Manager (Full-Timers) Meeting

Use manager meetings to: CHECK ACTIVITY ... presentations, policy pick-ups and recruits. Also hold manager meetings to TRAIN and MOTIVATE.

Tips:

No. 1 - Sell the Dream.
No. 2 - The "Top Priority" of this meeting is to "check activity" (especially field training activity).
No. 3 - Review goals and set plan of action for upcoming week.
No. 4 - Discuss "Good News" in ALW.
No. 5 - Recognize your people ... ask a leader who is "doing it" to stand up and speak.
No. 6 - Have role-playing sessions to help your people in their "weak" areas.
No. 7 - Keep this meeting short. This is a "business-type" meeting.

Training Sessions

Training sessions are for: BUILDING CRUSADERS and GETTING MAD at the competition:

No. 1 - Teach people how to sell the dream and how to become crusaders.
No. 2 - Discuss how to:

- Give a winning presentation
- Get a commitment
- Get husband and wife to client night
- Get referrals
- Recruit
- Prospect
- Field train
- Use third party material
- Sell A.L. Williams promotion guidelines
- Prepare for agents from competing companies
- Analyze policies
- Sell the $250 licensing and training reimbursement

No. 3 - Cover fundamentals:

- Disadvantages of cash value insurance (especially new kinds of Universal Life and Variable Life)
- How to sell enough protection
- Purpose of life insurance
- Common Sense Term
- Conditional receipt
- Theory of decreasing responsibility
- Dividends
- Why one policy per family
- Why no child policies
- Three things wrong with cash value insurance
- What is waiver of premium
- Why not load up policy with options (like accidental death)
- Field underwriting
- Magic of compound interest

No. 4 - A.L. Williams philosophy:

- ALW Way book
- Pushing Up People
- Common Sense book
- Positive attitude
- Recognition
- Treat people right
- No pressure
- No sale on first interview
- Always do what's best for client
- Do it first

No "Gotchas"

"At A.L. Williams, we want every person who has any relationship with the company to have a good feeling about it."
—Art Williams

Remember, your reputation is everything. Every person you touch will go away with either a POSITIVE or a NEGATIVE image of A.L. Williams.

Our sales and recruiting philosophies assure that everyone who associates with A.L. Williams will have a positive feeling about our company.

You should make sure YOUR ORGANIZATION maintains that image.

We have so many positives in A.L. Williams.

- We save people money or give them more value for the same money.
- We offer an opportunity with practically "no risk."
- Reimbursement plan (if recruit qualifies).
- No pressure to come full-time. You have a choice.
- No sale on the first interview (low-key approach).
- Unique "sales management" concept.
- Aggressive, can-do attitude.
- "Buy term and invest the difference in an IRA" - the best insurance and investment concept in the industry.
- Put the human factor back into business. We treat people good and put them first in company decisions.
- Replacement concept - we reward people for helping others succeed.
- Spouse involvement program - husband and wife partnership.

- A company built for "average" people. No requirements of education background, IQ, family status, etc. We accept people as they are.
- Best part-time opportunity in America.
- Opportunity for total financial independence.
- Built company that's good for consumers, good for salespeople.

BUILD PEOPLE, NOT SALES

IN THIS SECTION:

- Build People, Not Sales
- The Two "Laws" of Building People
- Beware of Traditional Management
- Treat People Good
- The One Thing People Want Most
- Pushing Up People
- Give to Your People
- Accept People for Who and What They Are
- Never Stop Believing in People
- You Do It First
- Commitment is a Two-Way Street
- What You Do Today Pays Off in Two or Three Years
- Your Reputation is Everything
- Work for Your People

- Don't lead by Intimidation
- Recognize Your People
- Pass Negatives Up, Positives Down
- Local Success
- Don't Loan Money
- Recognition: the Secret to Winning
  Steps to a Winning Recognition Program
- Praise Your People
- Tips For Praising People
- Use the Phone for Recognition
- Written Recognition
- Leaders Bulletins
- Recognizing with Awards
- Conventions

Build People, Not Sales

"It's important for a leader to understand what's unique about the sales management business."
—Art Williams

What's bad about sales?

You're unemployed every day.

What's good about sales?

It's the best way for the average person to earn a big income.

But ...

A great leader also knows that the key to success is not:

Building sales **or**

Building income

The key to great success is building people.

The Two "Laws" of Building People

No. 1 - The "Golden Rule"

"Do unto others as you would have them do unto you."

Be the kind of leader you would like to have.

No. 2 - Common Sense

Don't get "fancy" and try to use tactics and psychology. You don't have to be an expert - just use your good old common sense in dealing with people.

Your sense of right and wrong is a better guide than all the "management" books in the world

Don't Ask:

How many sales did you make?

How much premium did you do this week?

Do Ask:

How do you feel about the business?

How bad do you want to be somebody?

What can I do to help you?

Beware of "Traditional" Management

What universities and management schools teach:

1) Always put the "bottom line" first.
2) Keep a "professional distance" from people.
3) Don't let emotion be a part of business.

Wrong, Wrong, Wrong!!
A.L. Williams believes:

1) Always put people first.
2) Build personal relationships with your people.
3) Let your emotions show - love your people and let them know it.

Every great leader I've know has been EMOTIONAL. Get INVOLVED with your people! Put the "Human Factor" first in your business!!

Treat People Good

"You can't gain people's respect by treating them like numbers on a sales chart. If you want respect, you've got to show them that you care about them as people."
—Art Williams

No. 1 - Lead with positives, not negatives.

People do respect a strong, committed leader. They respond best to encouragement and support.

People don't respect a tyrant. They respond worst to intimidation and threats.

Remember: people give back what they get. Give people positives and they'll respond with positive action. Give them negatives and they'll respond with negative action.

No. 2 - Treat everyone equally.

People DO respect a leader who maintains a standard of excellence and judges them on their level of performance.

People DON'T respect a leader who discriminates against them on the basis of sex, race or background.

Remember: A great leader never "plays favorites" in ANYWAY.

The One Thing People Want Most

TO BE SOMEBODY!!

"Make me feel special."

"Make me feel important."

"I want to be somebody."

THE SINGLE MOST IMPORTANT CHARACTERISTIC FOR SUCCESS

It's **not** ability.

It's **not** education.

It's **not** family background.

IT IS DESIRE

... To be somebody

... To do something special with your life

... To make your family proud

Pushing Up People

"At A.L. Williams, you succeed by helping other people succeed. The more people you help, the more success you have. Pushing up people is a way of life at A.L. Williams."
—Art Williams

No. 1 - You cannot succeed alone.

- The more people you HELP MAKE MONEY, the more money YOU make.

No. 2 - You cannot earn promotions alone. The more people you help earn promotions, the more promotions you receive.
No. 3 - A leader always works for his people. Your people never "work for you."

Rules in our "Pushing Up People" concept:

No. 1 - Put yourself "last" ...

Don't talk about what "I" want

No. 2 - Never ask your people to work hard so you can win a promotion, contest, etc ...

Example ... Never have a contest so you can get a promotion, win a trip, etc .... Always have an attitude of helping your people get their promotion and then their success will help you get YOUR promotion!

No. 3 - Never be more concerned about your paycheck - be more concerned about their income ....

If your people make money, you make money.

No. 4 - Never make a management decision based on how it affects your income ....

Always do what is best for your people!

No. 5 - Never do anything that would give your people a reason to think you are trying to "hold them back."

Example ... Always look for a way to give your people credit for something so they can earn a promotion.

Give to Your People

"If you learn the 'giving principle,' I don't believe you will ever reach a level of success where you can no longer grow."
—Art Williams

The giving principle is the key to moving forward in your business career and in your life. Some people reach a certain level of success, then just stop. Usually, that's because they've stopped "giving" to others and withdrawn into themselves.

No. 1 - Don't be consumed by "selfness"

Live for others, not for yourself. Never stop giving:

- Give your commitment
- Give your loyalty
- Give your enthusiasm and support
- See your people as a joy, not a threat

No. 2 - Practice the "giving principle"

- The more you give, the more you will receive
- A giving person draws strength from those he seeks to help
- Give people a second and third chance
- Never get too busy to care about others

No. 3 - Give without expecting something in retum

- Follow the principle of "It's better to give than to receive."
- Give from the heart - you must be sincere.

Remember: The greater your capacity to give, the greater your personal success in business.

Accept People for Who and What They Are

"A leader must realize that you can't change people. You must accept them for who and what they are. A leader's job is to build on people's strengths and ignore their weaknesses."
—Art Williams

No. 1 - Don't judge people. Instead ...

- Encourage them.
- Motivate them.
- Love them.

No. 2 - Look for the reason behind negative attitudes.

People are negative for a reason. Don't just get mad and frustrated if someone seems negative. Look for the reasons why:

- They aren't winning.
- They don't have enough confidence.
- They don't have an example of success to follow.
- They aren't excited.

Then, look for what you can do to help.

No. 3 - Realize that everyone is different.

- Different people have different strengths and weaknesses.
- Some people need more encouragement than others.
- Nobody's perfect.

Allow for mistakes and help people to learn and grow from them. Concentrate on building personal relationships ALL THE TIME.

Never Stop Believing in People

"The only sure way for your people to lose is if they give up. Your lack of encouragement should never be the reason a person quits. A leader must always keep believing in people, no matter what."
—Art Williams

No. 1 - Have confidence in your people.

- See each person as a winner.
- Expect success from everyone.
- Let people know you think they can win.

No. 2 - Recognize each accomplishment, no matter how small:

- Show people that you know what they do.
- Make each small accomplishment seem major - it really is.
- Make your praise public - people love to be recognized among their peers.

No. 3- Sell the dream, again.

- Never think you can stop "selling the dream."
- People need to be constantly reminded of the rewards of their hard work.
- Encourage people to talk about their personal goals and dreams. (You could have a "dream" session and ask each person to tell his personal "success dream.")

No. 4 - Don't give up on people when they make mistakes.

- Live with them through the tough times, as well as the easy times.
- Care about each person as an individual.

- Allow people to learn from their mistakes. Never criticize.
- And ... Never be guilty of giving up AS A LEADER.

You Do It First

"A true leader always sets the standard for his people by doing it first. He never asks his people to do anything that he hasn't already done first."
—Art Williams

The greatest thing you can ever do for your people is prove:

- That they can win because you did
- That the nasty price is worth it because the rewards are so great
- That you (the leader) are the hardest worker, and HARD WORK OVERCOMES mistakes and "lack of talent," etc.

Remember: You always do first what you want your people to do

- If you recruit, your people will recruit
- If you make money, your people will make money
- If you are positive, your people will be positive

Commitment is a Two-Way Street

"Commitment must work both ways in order to achieve a successful relationship.
You must make a total commitment first.
Then, and only then, do you have a right to expect a commitment from your people."
—Art Williams

Most companies DEMAND a commitment from their people and FIRE or FORGET those same people when something goes wrong - they have problems, poor sales or recruiting or whatever.

A Leader's Commitment

If you want to be a leader in A.L. Williams, you must do the following:

No. 1 - Place no limits on your help and support

- Work with them as long as it takes for them to win.
- Field train with them as long as they need you.
- Be there for your people 24 hours a day, seven days a week.
- Provide your people with all the technical knowledge and support they need to get the job done.

No. 2 - Make an "unconditional" commitment

- Live with your people through good times and bad.
- Believe in them MORE than they believe in themselves.
- Be there for them when they do everything wrong.

No. 3 - Always be an example for your people to follow

- Work harder than anybody else (make more sales, recruit more people, make more sacrifices, do it better).
- Be more positive than anybody else.
- Love your job and "the crusade" more than anyone else.
- Make more money than anyone else.
- Be a better example in your personal life than anyone else.
- Be more ethical and honest than anyone else.

No. 4 - Your people's commitment to you

- Have good feelings about the company and the service they're providing for families.
- Believe in the crusade.
- Commit to the team and to helping the people they recruit to succeed.
- Give you and the company their best effort.

What You Do Today Pays Off in Two or Three Years

- The people you recruit today will take two or three years to develop.
- The sales you make one at a time, day by day, will make you "A Ton" two or three years from now.
- The people you build today will become champions two or three years from now.

And ..

- The mistakes you make today will show up two or three years from now.

Your Reputation is Everything

"A good reputation is better than gold. If people don't trust and believe in you, they'll never follow you."
—Art Williams

No. 1 - You must do what's right for consumers.

- Sell the right concept: "Buy term and invest the difference"
- Care more about the family than the sale:
  - No pressure
  - No sale on the first interview

No. 2 - You must do what's right for your people.

- Honor your commitments.
- Deliver on your promises.
- Put the "human factor" in every business situation.

No. 3 - You must set a personal example.

- Do whatever it takes.
  (There are no office hours for leaders.)

- Be involved. Work side by side with your people.
- You do it first.

People must see your success to believe it's possible for them.

Work for Your People

"Never ask your people to work hard so you can win a promotion, a contest, etc."
—Art Williams

A leader works for his people - his people DON'T work for him. You succeed in A.L. Williams by HELPING OTHERS SUCCEED.

- The more money your people make, the more money you earn.
- The more promotions your people get, the more promotions you earn.

You have CONTESTS to HELP YOUR PEOPLE EARN PROMOTIONS and their success will push you up AUTOMATICALLY.

'Pushing Up People" is a way of life in A.L. Williams.

Don't Lead By Intimidation

"Management by quotas, threats and intimidation will give you only 'short-range' results."
—Art Williams

Example:

Suppose you call a salesperson in who has had a bad month in sales and say, "If you don't double your sales this month, you're fired!"

He might go out and make the sales, but you have destroyed your relationship. People can't perform at their best under that kind of pressure.

But ...

Suppose you called that same person in and let him (or her) know that you BELIEVE in him. You sell the dream one more time. You make him FEEL GOOD about himself and his future. He will do 10 TIMES MORE business in that case than he would in a threatening environment like the one above.

Remember: You raise good leaders like you raise good children ... with praise, recognition and commitment.

Recognize Your People

"Before you can be a great leader,
you must master the art of recognition."
—Art Williams

People love to be "singled out."

- They hate to feel like "a number"
- Everyone needs recognition for a job well-done
- Recognition fills an "inner need" to be admired and appreciated

People respond better to praise than to punishment.

- You raise successful leaders like you raise successful kids
- You can't change people's personalities
- Accept people's weakness and praise their strengths
- Don't criticize

Recognition is the greatest motivator.

- People respond best to POSITIVE MOTIVATION Most companies manage by threat and intimidation
- Pushing Up People is the best kind of management

How to recognize your people:

No. 1 - Recognize 20-25% of the people at your meetings, no matter how large or small.
No. 2 - Don't spend a lot of money.

Use t-shirt awards, certificates, etc.
Write letters of praise

Make phone calls to people who are doing well
Do a special leaders sheet for your organization

No. 3 - Personalize each award.

Say a few things about each person who receives an award - something personal about him and his accomplishments

---

No. 4 - Create your own special awards.

I've used "Big Jock" awards, "I Am A Stud" awards, 6-foot trophies, etc.

No. 5 - Always include the partners.

Special, individual partners awards should be given at every meeting where others are recognized

---

No. 6 - Recognize some people who have "slipped".

Don't forget the people with great potential who have had a setback Let them know you recognize their potential. It should be positive and encouraging. I've used "Torn Sweater" awards, "Flash in the Pan" awards, etc.

No. 7 - Have fun.

Recognition ceremonies should be FUN - something your people look forward to

No. 8 - You can never give too much recognition.

Pass Negatives Up, Positives Down

"A leader's responsibility is to help eliminate people's problems and make them feel good."
—Art Williams

People will not follow a NEGATIVE, DULL, DISILLUSIONED, FRUSTRATED CRYBABY.

People WILL follow a person who is always POSITIVE, always "UP," always "CHARGING."

Your job as a leader ...

No. 1 - Relieve your people of their problems.

You must be a kind of "FATHER" FIGURE to your people. LISTEN to all their problems, REASSURE them they can be solved, ENCOURAGE them and SELL THE DREAM again.

People won't buy from or come to work with a negative, frustrated person. You must let your people "DUMP ALL THE NEGATIVES" on you. When you do, they leave your office feeling more positive and confident, and those feelings lead to more success in their work.

No. 2 - You can't always tell people what you really think about them.

Sometimes people will complain to you about what seem like minor problems. Sometimes you can see that the reason they're not doing well is that they're just not making the effort. A leader can get tired of listening to a lot of "petty" problems or trying to solve disagreements between two people in the office.

BUT. . .You can't ever "lose your cool." You can't give in to the urge to tell people what you think their faults are.

Remember: Your job is to always "push people up."

- Take every problem seriously. No problem is really "minor" if it is causing a person to be upset and non-productive.
- Don't criticize or be negative. Remember: You can say 99 positive things and one negative thing and the person will only remember the one negative.
- Every person has some good qualities. Everybody has done something right. Talk about the things the person does right and encourage activity in the poor areas. Let the person know you still believe in him or her.

No. 3 - Never pass your problems down to your people.

You can't burden your people with YOUR problems. It's lonely at the top, but that's the price of being a leader.

TAKE YOUR PROBLEMS "UP." Talk to your upline when you're upset or discouraged. He or she will fill the same role for you that you do for your people.

Discussing your problems with those below you

will only discourage and worry them. They have their own problems, and a "troubled" leader will only burden them more.

Remember: Set an example of excitement, enthusiasm and concern for your people. They need your help and support to become the best they can be!

Local Success

"It is not good enough for company leaders only to be successful. You must have local success before your people will believe."
—Art Williams

You must have someone in your organization succeed (make money, save money, earn promotions, be at the top of the Leaders Bulletin, win contests), before your people will believe the opportunity is real.

That someone should be you!

Don't Loan Money

"I believe that, when you loan money, you only help people 'put off' solving their problems."
—Art Williams

I have loaned well over $100,000 to people in my career, but I have never loaned anyone any money that did not have to borrow MORE money later on.

I believe that loaning people money ONLY DELAYS A PROBLEM. make A COMMITMENT like this:

I will give you everything I've got- my ATTITUDE, my EXPERIENCE, my ABILITY, my TOUGHNESS, but I WON'T do TWO THINGS for you:

No. 1 - I won't loan you money, because that's not the answer to your problems.
No. 2 - I won't quit with you. A.L. Williams is it for me, and I won't help you "give up."

Recognition: The Secret To Winning

"Motivating people is the secret to being a great leader."
—Art Williams

Recognition is one of the most powerful forms of motivation.

If you can learn how to recognize people, reward them, and make them feel like they are "somebody," then you will have found the secret to winning in A.L. Williams.

No. 1 - People are starving for recognition. They want someone to notice them and someone to tell them that "who they are" and "what they do" matters.

No. 2 - Recognition works because people want to prove to others that the recognition is deserved.

- If your upline leader tells you that you are doing a GREAT job recruiting, you tend to work that much harder at recruiting.
- If your upline leader recognizes you in front of 1000 people as best field trainer, you tend to work that much harder at field training.

No. 3 - If you have a great recognition program, your people will want to come to work.

No. 4 - Recognition builds personal relationships.

Steps To A Winning Recognition Program

"You have a responsibility to set up a recognition program for your people."

—Art Williams

There are already forms of recognition in A.L. Williams. There are awards, conventions, Leaders Bulletins, On Targets, etc. But that is not enough.

YOU MUST BUILD YOUR OWN "RECOGNITION PROGRAM."

Step 1 - Think of yourself as a leader.

If you perceive yourself as a true leader, then what you say when you recognize others will matter.

Step 2 - Realize that there is no such thing as "too much" recognition.

A person never outgrows his need for recognition.

Step 3 - Take the responsibility to reach the newest people in your organization.

Don't count on someone else to "do it."

Step 4 - In the beginning, a "recognition program" should be simple and cost nothing.
(See "Praise Your People," page 28)
Step 5 - Get started now.

Praise Your People

"The simplest and best way to recognize people is to tell them they've done a good job."
—Art Williams

The key to recognizing people isn't trips or fur coats alone. By themselves, these rewards mean little. It's the simple things you say and do that matter to people.

No. 1 - Never miss a chance to tell someone he is doing something right.

Example:

A person feels great when you stand at the podium in front of a lot of people and praise him. You might say, "Here is a stud who really knows how to do this business."

No. 2 - Help people improve in certain areas by complimenting them the right way.

Example:

Someone needs to become better at giving the Asset Management presentation. Look for ways to compliment him on his presentation. Chances are he will become encouraged and try even harder to improve.

No. 3 - Always pass positives down.

Look for ways to encourage people. Praising people is fun.

Remember: In most of the corporate world, the boss is great about pointing out mistakes.

People make mistakes - it's only human. But you never get anywhere by criticizing your people.

Tips For Praising People

No. 1 - At Opportunity Meetings.

- Circulate through the crowd and introduce yourself. If you meet a "sharp" guest, find the person who brought him and say, "That person is SHARP! You did a great job getting him here. Keep bringing people like that!"

- Ask a person to stand up and recognize him for his great attitude.

No. 2 - After a sale

- After a recruit's first sale, congratulate him in front of others.

No. 3 - At Fast Start Schools

- Call people up to the front, announce their income and shake their hands.
- Ask all the RVPs in the room to come up and congratulate a person who is "doing it."

No. 4 - At manager meetings

- Ask top producers to come to the front of the room. Ask them to bring their spouse to the front.

No. 5 - Ask about the family

- Ask about a person's spouse or child by name.

No. 6 - Have an audience

- Praise a person in front of as many people as possible. This makes others want to work for the same praise and makes the person you recognize feel that much better.

No. 7 - Set up special appointments

- Call the husband and wife in for a special appointment, just to talk to them and encourage them. Sell the dream. Ask them to list goals. Challenge them to accomplish something. Let them know you are excited about what they are doing. Tell them A.L. Williams is for real.

Use The Phone For Recognition

"When phoning your people, remember that sales and premium cannot be controlled. Attitude and activity can."
—Art Williams

Using the phone is one of the easiest ways to recognize people. Do you call your downline people on a regular basis?

- Select one night a week for calling your people.
- Never ask: "How many sales?" or "How much premium?"

If a person has no sales, he will feel bad enough! Besides, if he DID have any sales, you can be sure he will tell you anyway!

Instead: "How are things going?" "What kind of people are you recruiting?" "Hang in there!" "I'm proud to have you on our team!" "You have a fantastic attitude!"

Always return phone calls.

Written Recognition

"Everyone loves to get mail and they love to get letters praising their efforts."
—Art Williams

The greatest leaders in A.L. Williams take time out every day to write a personal letter to at least one person.

- Sit down right now and write five short notes to people who really deserve it.

Example:

Joe,

No matter what happens, don't let the little things get you down. Just hang in there.

A.L. Williams is going to deliver. Joe, I'm proud to have you on our team.

- Write personal, handwritten letters as much as possible.
- Send form letters with a handwritten note at the bottom.
- Ask a leader to write a letter to his or her spouse, thanking that spouse for understanding and support. Then read the letter to the whole group at a meeting.

Don't mention who it's to or from until the end.

- Write to Art or an NSD and say how great one of your people is doing. At the bottom of the page write: cc: Joe Stud. Then send the letter to the upline leader and a copy to the downline manager.
- When you hear someone speak highly of another person, tell that other person what you heard.

Leaders Bulletins

"A.L. Williams people love to compete."
—Art Williams

Ranking your people is an important part of recognition. The Leaders Bulletin from the home office is not enough.

Purpose: To encourage healthy competition and make sure everyone knows about activity.

- Always have a leaders bulletin for your organization.
- Start out with a 1-page, typewritten bulletin.
- Highlight "heroes" on the bulletin.
- Make headlines from fancy print in magazines and newspapers.
- Set up a bulletin board or a grease board in your office area. Rank your leaders on these boards and update daily.

Leaders sheets, bulletins and poster boards are simple to do and are always successful.

If you are a sales leader or district with a small organization, consider clustering your rankings with someone else.

Recognizing With Awards

"It's not what you give, but how you give it."
—Art Williams

Plan to recognize 20-25% of the people in attendance; more, if the group is small.

T-shirts:

- The "best" award. Grown men who make $75,000 a year have gone back home and cried because they didn't get at-shirt.
- Use t-shirts to create unity; special colors separate "RVPs" from "District Leaders," "Sales Leaders," etc.
- "I ain't average," "I am somebody," "I want Pru BAD," "RVP or Bust," etc.

Buttons

- 2-3" in diameter
- Use to recognize recruiting or activity
- Give out at Fast Start Schools

Certificates:

- Write name and award in calligraphy
- Frame in inexpensive frame

Hats:

- Print title on bill of hat

“Fun Awards:”

- A “big banana” for the top producer
- A “bunch of grapes” for the top recruiter

'Prestige” Awards:

- Watches
- Special blazers
- Jeweled pins
- Leader bars

Unsigned Check Award:

- Mail an unsigned check to a spouse in your organization with a letter explaining that the spouse can spend the check any way he or she likes once the check is signed.

Explain that you will sign the check when the licensed spouse picks up five sets of policies in the next four weeks.

Plaques:

- Have a "rotating" award that is passed from top producer each month. Have last month's winner present the award to this month's winner. Inscribe new winner's name on the rotating plaque and keep plaque in the reception area.
- Give plaques for: RVP of the month, Most PPUs, Top Recruiter, Top in Submitted Premium
- Always explain the award and why you are giving it
- Plan to recognize 20-25% of the people in attendance
- Always include spouse's name on plaque
- Display plaques in a prominent place in the office
- Teasing Recognition: Recognition should be fun, but never a "put down." If you give a "turkey of the month" or a "torn sweater," be sure you are recognizing a true superstar who can do better, usually a person who has already won positive recognition.

Conventions

"The ultimate way to sell the dream."
—Art Williams

Rules:

No. 1 - Don't spend beyond your means!
No. 2 - Hold contest to qualify for conventions
No. 3 - Include part-timers! (First A.L. Williams conventions were for part-timers as well as managers.)
No. 4 - Recognize at least 25% of your people.
No. 5 - Never plan a "trip for two." Convention should be for as many of your people as possible.
No. 6 - Base contest on 1) submitted premium and 2) income 4 ways to finance conventions:

- RVP is responsible for getting a place that is "impressive" but "very inexpensive."
  - Price should not keep anyone from attending

— No one should worry about the cost after they have attended

- RVP pays all costs (more or less) based on production. Top people attend free-of-charge
- RVP pays all costs for top people, next levels pay certain amounts
- RVP pays for awards, handouts, and maybe one awards banquet. Everyone pays for air travel and other costs.

No. 7 - Get input from your management team! Delegate responsibility.

No. 8 - Negotiate with hotel for prices.

No. 9 - Include spouses in planning and in your recognition.

No. 10 - Plan "retreats" at "out-of-the-way" resorts ... 1 1/2 to 3 days maximum.

No. 11 - Always allow "free time" for fellowship.

LEADERSHIP ATTITUDES

IN THIS SECTION:

- Three Kinds of Leaders
- We Believe in Doing What's Right
- Building Trust
- Give Your People Credit for the Team's Success
- Partner Power
- It's Not What, But When
- Always Be Good
- Screwed-Up Thinking
- No Place for Prejudice
- Remember the Human Touch
- Contradictions
- Your "Position" as a Leader
- "Do It"
- You Must "Love" A.L. Williams
- A Company Where Salespeople Are King
- Prestige vs. Opportunity
- The Free Enterprise System
- We Reward the Right Kind of Person
- A Better way to Market Term Insurance
- The ALW Uniform
- Top Priority
- Face-To-Face

- No Pressure
- Greenies
- No Risk
- Unlimited Number of RVP Positions
- No "Junior" RVPs
- Can't Wear Two Hats
- This is a Numbers Business
- Be Slow to Recommend Termination
- When Do You Recommend Termination?
- Bringing Part-Timers Full-Time
- Buying a MILICO Policy
- Recruit
- Field Training
- Average Size Policy
- Steps to Winning
- Always Be Positive
- Get Your Priorities Straight
- Three Stages of Commitment
- Desire Is the Key
- Most People Almost Do Enough to Win
- You Must Become a Dreamer Again
- "Forbidden" Words

- Time
- The “Little” Things Make “the Difference”
- Always Be Excited
- Don’t Feel Guilty
- Avoid Panic Management
- Charge!
- Expect to Win
- You Must Pay a Price
- Think Big - Don’t Major in Minor Things
- Surge
- The Magic of “90 Days”
- Hang Tough
- The Magic of “Working Hard”
- Don’t Let Fear Stop You!
- Impatient for Success
- A Little Bit More
- Always Play Scared
- Work Two or More Levels Below You
- Excuses Don’t Count
- Fight
- Always Be Willing to Start Over
- All You Can Do Is All You Can Do

Three Kinds of Leaders

No. 1 - Winners ...

are people who are frustrated and scared every day. They want to quit every day. They hurt, cry and worry every day - just like everybody else.

BUT, winners are OBSESSED. They are MADMEN. In spite of their frustrations and fears, they go out every day and win ....

No. 2 - Potential winners ...

These are people who have a chance to be a winner. They wake up every day frustrated, scared and worried just like the winner. But they don't go out and compete, primarily because they don't know what to do.

These people have a chance if they learn the A.L. Williams Way.

No. 3 - Losers ...

'These people wake up every day with the same doubts, fears and worries of the winner and potential winners. They are humans just like everyone else.

But they won't work or compete. They don't even really care. They take advantage of their people and their company. They can't believe in anything or anybody (especially themselves). These people want something for nothing.

They don't have a chance.

We Believe in Doing What's Right

We've got a philosophy- and it's not just "talk." We live by it ...

- We believe in "buy term and invest the difference."
- We believe in the "theory of decreasing responsibility."
- We believe that inexpensive, permanent term life insurance gives consumers the most value for their insurance dollar.

- We believe in selling term life insurance 100% of the time.
- We believe in selling "in person," one-on-one across the kitchen table.
- We believe in the 3-step sales process- we never sell on a first interview.
- We believe in selling the consumer what we believe in owning on our own lives.
- We believe that IRAs and Keoghs are the best investments available in America today.
- We believe in giving the consumer a chance to compare life insurance products and make the best decision for his family.

Building Trust

"To be a great leader, you must believe in the goodness of people."
—Art Williams

Trust in people is a quality that all true leaders possess. It's not always easy. There will always be some "LOS-

ERS" who will hurt you and your team, abuse your trust and turn against you.

The challenge to a leader is to not let the losers, the negative people, the unethical people and the dishonest people make you lose faith in people.

If you lose your ability to trust, you've lost your effectiveness as a leader.

Remember ...

- 99% of the people are good, decent, honest and caring.
- You can't let the 1% change you and make you negative.
- You must always look for the "good things" in people.
- MUTUAL TRUST IS THE QUALI1Y THAT TURNS AN "ORGANIZATION" INTO A "TEAM."

Give Your People Credit for the Team's Success

"A true leader gives to his people. When he fails, he blames himself. And when he wins, he gives the credit to others."
—Art Williams

The head coach must always operate by the following two rules:

No. 1 - Always give your team, your leaders and/or your RVPs "credit" for your success and the team's success.
No. 2 - You always take "the blame" when things go wrong. The leader is responsible for everything that happens.

Remember: Always take every opportunity to let everybody know how great your people really are.

Partner Power

"A husband and wife committed to a joint goal can accomplish a ton more than any one person."
—Art Williams

Don't forget to include the Partner in every area of your business. The Partner can make a difference in "success or failure."

Areas of importance:

No. 1 - Make sure the spouse is at the kitchen table when you present the concept and close the sale ...

No. 2 - Get the spouse to the Client Night, Orientation Meeting Fast Start School and Partner's meeting.

No. 3 - Recognize and reward the spouse and the Partner's organization ....

Remember: A person's spouse has more influence than anyone else in his life.

It's Not What, But When

"It's not good enough just to know what to do,
it's when you do it that really counts."
—Art Williams

I believe that TIMING is the key to building a successful business.

Building a team and working with people is very complex. Every individual is different. You must develop GREAT INSTINCTS and FEELINGS. You must know JUST THE RIGHT TIME to make a move.

For Example:

No. 1 - You can be a master at making people feel special, but if one of your people is having a personal crisis and you're not there with the right word at just the right time - you've failed!

No. 2 - You can be a great recruiter, but if one of your key recruits quits and you don't immediately go out and recruit two or three more to replace him - you've failed!

No. 3 - You can be great at making a huge income, but if you don't save money and prepare for an emergency - you've failed!

Always Be Good

"In order to be a good leader, you must be a good person."
—Art Williams

The tendency for many people when they achieve a certain level of success is for them to become a different person.

They reach a "comfort zone" and then decide that they don't have to get their hands "dirty." They believe they don't have to keep doing the "tough" things like building personal relationships with new people and personally recruiting and field training.

You should never let success change you and make

you an arrogant person. If you do, you will no longer be an effective leader.

Instead,

No. 1 - Remember where you came from

You didn't get to the top without the help of a lot of other people who may still be struggling

No. 2 - Always be a good, caring person

People won't buy you as a leader unless they know you care

Screwed-Up Thinking

"A leader has a responsibility to wake up everyday and do something to help his people win and help his business get better."
—Art Williams

There are "3 Classic Mistakes" many leaders make in their thinking:

No. 1 - If you think your people owe you for what you did for them, your career is "already headed downhill."
No. 2 - If you think the company owes you for what you did in the past, you are already being "a has been."
No. 3 - If you get up every morning and think it's "good enough" to just "not do anything illegal," to not make any mistakes, you are "already a loser."

"Winners concentrate on winning,
and losers concentrate on getting by..."
—Art Williams

No Place for Prejudice

"In A.L. Williams, a person's success is based entirely on performance, regardless of his sex, race or background."
—Art Williams

There is no place for prejudice in A.L. Williams. For example, we have many women leaders who have built incredible careers and incomes through high production and outstanding leadership qualities. They are judged, just like everyone else in the company, by a standard of excellence instead of standards like male and female, black and white and so forth.

In A.L. Williams, that is THE ONLY STANDARD for promotions and recognition.

Remember: Our computer can't discriminate. It "pays" you for good business and you receive "chargebacks" for bad business.

Remember the Human Touch

"The more personal contact you have with people, the more successful you will become."
—Art Williams

There is no substitute in this business for personal contact.

I believe there are at least four areas in which personal contact is critical:

No. 1 - Prospecting

Telephones and letters are an ineffective means of prospecting because they LACK CREDIBILITY. No one respects a person who calls him on the phone or sends him a letter. There is COMPLETE CREDIBILITY in "going by" with someone to see people in a warm market.

People trust you more when they can see your face.

No. 2 - Field training

One hour of field training is better than 10 hours in a classroom ....

No. 3 - Managing your organization

You must spend as much time with your people as you can. You must inspect them "eyeball-to-eyeball." Meet with them late at night after they come out of the field. Spend time with them at social gatherings on the weekend.

The "human touch" is more effective than any other means of management. It shows people you CARE.

No. 4 - With clients

After you have sold someone a policy, meet with him as much as you possibly can when he needs your help. It will show him that you CARE about HIM, and not just about selling him insurance. You may also INCREASE your chances of RECRUITING HIM.

Contradictions

"Great leaders must learn to be flexible. They must understand the contradictions of the business world and develop the ability to accept contradictions and still work effectively."
—Art Williams

When you're working with people and building a big organization, you will see many things CONTRADICT what you thought were ABSOLUTES.

I believe that it is your ability to deal with these contradictions and NOT LOSE FAITH in your philosophies and beliefs that will DETERMINE THE SUCCESS YOU WILL HAVE in A.L. Williams.

Examples:

No. 1 - Freedom

A.L. Williams gives you unbelievable freedom to build "a company within a company" when you become an RVP. But, you can't put yourself above the team. That freedom carries with it an equal amount of responsibility. In order to "live up" to your responsibilities, you must sacrifice some freedom to never do anything to destroy or hurt our company and its people.

No. 2 - Positive Attitude

You must always be positive and give and give and give. But, sometimes a person comes along and takes advantage of A.L. Williams and their own people. At that time, you may have to "come down tough" on them or maybe even terminate them. Still, you can NEVER let those people change you and make you negative.

Remember: Don't ever give up on the principles and traditions of A.L. Williams.

Your "Position" as a Leader

"Many leaders think their 'position' makes them something special. Positions don't count - people do."
—Art Williams

Leadership Key: A position doesn't make a person, a person makes a position.

As a leader ...

- You can't DEMAND respect
- You can't DEMAND loyalty
- You can't DEMAND trust
- You can't DEMAND love

You have to earn it!

As a leader ...

- You can't FAKE honesty
- You can't FAKE integrity
- You can't FAKE belief

You must be sincere!

As a leader, it's not good enough just to be right, your people must BELIEVE you're right before you can gain their trust and respect.

"Do It"

"The winners do it and do it and keep on doing it until they win."
—Art Williams

Almost is a way of life to almost everybody.

- ALMOST everybody ALMOST works hard enough.
- ALMOST everybody is ALMOST committed enough.
- ALMOST everybody ALMOST sacrifices enough.
- ALMOST everybody ALMOST recruits enough.
- ALMOST everybody ALMOST saves enough.

But ...
The winners "do it!"
What do they do?

They "do it" and "do it" and "do it" and "do it" and "do it'· and "do it" UNTIL THEY WIN.

You Must "Love" A.L. Williams

No. 1 - You can't like "buy tenn and invest the difference" and win.
No. 2 - You can't like "the theory of decreasing responsibility" and win.
No. 3 - You can't like doing what's right for families and win.
No. 4 - You can't like your people and win.
No. 5 - You can't like "the A.L. Williams Way" and win.
No. 6 -You must "love" A.L. Williams and the things we stand for.

Remember: Crusaders die hard!

A Company Where Salespeople Are King

*"A.L. Williams was built by salespeople,
for salespeople."
—Art Williams*

Most corporations in American business are run by lawyers, accountants, business graduates and so on. In A.L. Williams, salespeople ONLY "call the shots."

We believe that ONLY SALESPEOPLE CAN RUN A SALES COMPANY. Unless you've carried a briefcase and "had your nose bloodied" out there in the field, facing rejection and fighting the competition, you can't possibly understand what this business is all about.

A.L. WILLIAMS is COMMITTED to giving the people in sales- the ones who FIGHT THE COMPETITION ON THE FRONT LINES EVERY DAY - all the GREAT RESPONSIBILITIES and all the GREAT REWARDS.

Prestige vs. Opportunity

"At AL. Williams, we offer a for real opportunity."
—Art Williams

A.L. Williams was built to give a different kind of man and woman a chance to be somebody.

No true leader in A.L. Williams ever over-promotes our opportunity. It is NOT EASY to earn $100,000 a year. It is NOT EASY to build a successful business. We don't believe in "something for nothing" or "get rich quick."

You win at A.L. Williams by paying an "ugly price."

I don't want A.L. Williams to be like many companies in America and give their people a fancy title, nice office, a country club membership, but no opportunity.

We aren't interested in PRESTIGE. You get prestige after you WIN.

A CORNERSTONE of A.L. Williams:

A position doesn't make a person, but a person makes a position.

All a company can and should do for you

is give you a "For Real" Opportunity. But we won't and can't do it for you.

You can make your opportunity what it is - special or very average.

The Free Enterprise System

"The free enterprise system is the greatest system in the world. It's the cornerstone of "the A.L. Williams way."
—Art Williams

Many companies in the United States are SOCIALISTIC in their thinking. They believe that you should LIMIT THE OPPORTUNITY of the most capable people and keep everyone at the same income level. They don't allow the individual the opportunity to do something really great.

Many companies believe in TAKING FROM THE STUDS and GIVING TO THE DUDS, the people who haven't "done it."

DEAD WRONG!!

A.L. Williams believes in giving EVERYONE great opportunity. We believe in REWARDING THE STUDS that "do it" in a special way. We give EVERYONE an equal opportunity to PAY THE PRICE and W1N.

I believe that a company achieves GREATER GROWTH and provides a BETTER OPPORTUNITY if you put NO LIMITS on those special people who "do it big." If those top leaders keep getting better, keep breaking records and keep earning more, EVERYBODY WINS!

That's how it is in the FREE ENTERPRISE SYSTEM, the best system in the world today.

We Reward the Right Kind of Person

"Brains don't win in A.L. Williams. Hard work, excitement and 'want to' do."
—Art Williams

Common characteristics of our winners:

No. 1 - A good person
No. 2 - Unbelieveable desire to win

No. 3 - Tremendous faith in our system
No. 4 - Money motivated
No. 5 - Works hard
No. 6 - Has a positive attitude

A Better Way To Market Term Insurance

There are three reasons why part-time people make the difference for the consumer:

No. 1 - By hiring part-timers, we can hire a better quality person.

We find people who already have an income, so they don't have to use HIGH PRESSURE TACTICS or BE PUSHY AND AGGRESSIVE.

No. 2 - By hiring part-timers, our people can be "better trained" to work in the best interest of the client.

They don't feel the pressure of having to make a sale, because they already have a job and an income. They can afford to "take their time" and educate the client to "buy term and invest the difference."

Our TRAINING PROGRAM prepares our people to better serve the consumer.

We require our people to observe AT LEAST THREE TRAINING SALES- THAT'S A MINIMUM OF NINE CLIENT INTERVIEWS before they go out on their own.

No. 3 - Hiring part-time people is the most efficient way to get our product to the American consumer.

We don't have to pay high start-up salaries. We don't have the high initial costs that other companies do.

We don't have to spend millions on advertising because we have enough people to spend time "one-on-one" at the kitchen table.

Our people are stable in the community - they already have great contacts and they sell to their friends and community.

The ALW Uniform

"It is a privilege to wear our uniform."
—Art Williams

You ought to be PROUD to be in A.L. Williams. You should never feel like you have to beg people to buy a policy or beg people to come to work for us.

We have the GREATEST OPPORTUNITY in the world. We don't just sell policies; we save people's financial futures. We save them money. If people don't realize that, then it is THEIR LOSS, not YOURS.

"30% of the people reserve the right to remain stupid forever."

To be successful, you must be proud of what you do and be confident.

Top Priority

"A leader must never forget the two things that make A.L. Williams special - that we're crusaders and that we're dreamers."
—Art Williams

There are two keys to maintaining a positive attitude in your organization all the time.

No. 1 - Always sell "the crusade."

This is THE GLUE that holds your team together. Being a crusader gives a person the COURAGE necessary to "keep coming back."

No. 2 - Always sell "the dream."

Your job, as a leader, is to make your people FEEL GOOD and FEEL SPECIAL. Always selling THE DREAM keeps excitement, enthusiasm and an air of electricity in your organization.

Face-To-Face

"Everything you do in your business creates an impression - either good or bad. At A.L. Williams, we don't deal in 'tricks and gimmicks.' We deal with people one-on-one, face-to-face."
—Art Williams

- People don't like for a stranger to call them on the phone and invade their privacy.
- They don't like telephone machines calling them at home.
- They don't like being invited to meetings with no explanation of why they're going. We don't need that in A.L. Williams.
- At A.L. Williams, we're PROUD of our concept and our opportunity. We're not afraid to LOOK PEOPLE IN THE EYE and tell them about our business.
- People respect people who LOOK TALK and ACT like average, ordinary, good people. That's what we are, and that's how we want people to see our company. This is a "face-to-face" business!

- You've got to prospect FACE-TO-FACE ...
- You've got to recruit FACE-TO-FACE ...
- You've got to get referrals FACE-TO-FACE ...

Or you can't win "long-range" in this business.

No Pressure

"The life insurance industry has a particularly bad reputation of fast-talking, hard-closing, high-pressure sales. When we started A.L. Williams, we made a commitment that we were going to treat people like we wanted to be treated ourselves."
—Art Williams

When A.L. Williams was founded, we made a decision: **We will never sell on a first interview**

- At this company, we're not going to put people under pressure. We believe in taking an EDUCATIONAL APPROACH to this business.

The traditional industry ... has complicated and confused a simple business.

Our job ... is to simplify the business and help people understand what they need and what they're getting.

- We're NOT there just to sell policies.
- We ARE there to show people how to SAVE MONEY and to get MORE VALUE from their money.

Greenies

"A.L. Williams was built by recruiting greenies."
—Art Williams

We believe in building A.L. Williams with greenies.

We don't want:

- "Fancy" people
- "Prima donnas"
- Slick sales types

The best markets for recruiting "greenies:"

- Age 25 and up
- Married
- Children
- Own home
- Minimum income of $30,000

Important note: Two reasons not to recruit "traditional" salespeople:

- Poor reputation in community
- No warm market

No Risk

"We found a better way to build a company."
Art Williams

The insurance industry has a bad reputation of high pressure, fast talking and hard closing sales.

It is also known for a high turnover of agents (1/3 of

its agents drop out the first year, 2/3 by the end of the second year and 85% by the fourth year).

Because of this, most Americans can never see themselves selling life insurance. A.L. Williams found a BETTER WAY to attract a BETTER QUALITY PERSON in our industry.

Almost everyone in middle America needs EXTRA INCOME. A.L. Williams created the greatest part -time opportunity in America:

No. 1 - Professional- must have a license

- Not like selling soap, shoe polish, vitamins, etc.

No. 2 - Save people money

- Don't sell policies

No. 3 - No sale on the first interview

- No pressure

And practically no risk

A new recruit pays only his state licensing fee, test and course fees, plus a $25.00 processing fee. If a new recruit completes our training and licensing program, he is reimbursed $250, and he has not made a sale yet.

We want every person who has anything to do with A.L. Williams (client, part-timer, or full-timer) to feel good about our company.

Unlimited Number of RVP Positions

"Most companies have three or four 'top' positions. At A.L. Williams, we have an unlimited number of positions at the top."
—Art Williams

One of the most difficult decisions of a head football coach is picking the 11 BEST STARTERS. Many times you have 20-30 players who are dedicated, work hard, and are better than some players on the teams you compete against. But they are just at the wrong place at the wrong time.

That can NEVER, NEVER, NEVER happen at A.L.

Williams. We don't have just 11 first string positions, we have an UNLIMITED NUMBER of positions at the top - it all depends on YOUR efforts.

A.L. Williams judges all people ON THEIR OWN MERIT; people compete ONLY AGAINST THEMSELVES. They are promoted when they meet the requirements. A.L. Williams makes a commitment to each person that he or she will NEVER BE HELD BACK

Remember: A.L. Williams will never deny you an earned promotion.

No "Junior" RVPs

"The RVP position is the "backbone" of the A.L. Williams promotion system. It is at the RVP position that people are able to truly begin building their own business."
—Art Williams

No. 1 - There are no "junior" RVPs in A.L. Williams.

All RVPs are in business for themselves.

- They are responsible for running their business.
- They are responsible for motivating and leading their people.
- They are responsible for maintaining the image and reputation of A.L. Williams.
- They are responsible for the success or failure of their business.

No. 2 - All RVPs report only to their NSD or Art Williams.

Only exceptions

- Legal area
- Quality of business

In these two areas RVPs are responsible to their upline RVP or SVP to not do anything legally wrong and not to produce a poor quality business. RVPs are NOT required to attend meetings or conventions held by their upline RVP or SVP.

No. 3 - RVPs have an obligation to help "police" A.L. Williams.

All RVPs have a responsibility to report any violations of company policy or rules to their NSD or Art Williams. (We demand that our people do what is RIGHT for the company and for their people. The "good people" in our company must not be allowed to be hurt by those who would violate our principles or the RVP contract.)

Can't Wear Two Hats

"One person can only make so many sales. With our 'sales management concept,' we offer people the chance to make unlimited income."
—Art Williams

You must make a decision to be a LEADER or a SALESPERSON. You CANNOT do both and be successful.

I believe you should choose to be a LEADER for two reasons:

No. 1 - You can make unlimited income ...

There are only 24 hours in a day and one person can produce just so many sales.

No. 2 - You can build not only a large income, but also a secure income.

Salespeople are unemployed every day. If you don't wake up and prospect, you don't eat.

This Is a Numbers Business

"The only way to hire quality is to hire quantity."
—Art Williams

No. 1 - Experience is the greatest teacher in the world.

- The more you recruit, the better you get at recruiting.

No. 2 - This is a numbers business.

- The more people you recruit, the GREATER the ODDS of you finding that special person.
- General rule: 50 to 75 part-time recruits from your organization will earn your RVP promotion.

No. 3 - It only takes a few good producers and a lot of average producers to build an empire.

- A lot doing "a little bit," but a few doing "a bunch"

No. 4 - The key is not only how many you recruit, but what you do with those you do recruit.

- You must look at every recruit as an RVP trainee.

No. 5 - Try not to pick your winners too early.

Make your people earn promotions by production, not talk.

Be Slow to Recommend Termination

"Always give people a second, third, fourth and fifth chance."
—Art Williams

Most big companies are quick to terminate people who make a mistake or don't do everything right in their job.

I believe that EXPERIENCE is the greatest teacher. As a leader, you've got to allow your people to "screw up" sometimes, make mistakes and learn from them.

But ...

When that happens, the leader can't just TERMINATE them.

No. 1 - Give people the benefit of the doubt.

- If there's any question about what happened, give people the benefit of the doubt. Assume that they are doing their best and trying hard.
- Be slow to listen to other people. Study the situation and form your own opinions.

No. 2 - Keep "Pushing Up People."

- Keep believing in people, even when they screw up.
- Keep selling people the dream.
- Keep making people feel special.

When Do You Recommend Termination?

"No one is bigger than the team"
—Art Williams

There are a few exceptions in which termination is the only answer.

No. 1 - Illegal activity

You can't allow anyone on your team to jeopardize the reputation and future of A.L. Williams.

No. 2 - Serious attitude problems

You can't allow a bitter, negative person to destroy the attitude and energy of your entire organization. Counsel with this kind of person as much as you can. But, if his or her attitude is destroying your business, you must take action.

Remember: Nobody's bigger than the team.

You can't let anyone hurt the company and the opportunity.

RVPs and SVPs should make all recommendations for terminations to Williams, Inc.

Bringing Part-Timers Full-Time

"There's a right time for everything, including coming full-time at A.L. Williams."
—Art Williams

There are TWO ways to become financially independent in A.L. Williams:

No. 1 - By working part-time and investing your extra income
No. 2 - By working full-time and becoming a successful RVP

You should ALWAYS sell the Dream and talk about the positives of being an RVP.

But ....

Our goal at A.L. Williams is to improve a person's life. If A.L. Williams can help a person live a better life-style, that's all we want. People should come full-time ONLY when it's right for them and their families.

Remember:

- Never force a person to come full-time
  - It has to be right for THEM. Full-time requires a TOTAL COMMITMENT. YOU, as a leader, can't make that commitment for someone else.
- Never make that decision for anyone
  - It's a READY-MADE excuse for failure if a leader can "blame you" for "forcing" him to come full-time. There are a million excuses people give for quitting. If there is someone else to "blame," it's easy to quit.

Buying a MILICO Policy

"New A.L. Williams recruits should buy a MILICO policy if it fits their family's needs and they qualify for it."

—Art Williams

New A.L. Williams recruits don't have to buy a MILICO policy to come to work for our company.

- They should buy only if they have a need for insurance.
- If they desire to buy, they should buy based on their family's need.

However ...

New recruits should "practice what they preach" to their clients about insurance. If they don't believe in "buy term and invest the difference," they won't be able to sell it to others convincingly and honestly.

We don't want "phoneys" in A.L. Williams. If new recruits own or buy whole life insurance, and believe in it, they may not be suited to come to work for A.L. Williams.

Recruit

"Nothing excites an office like 'new blood.'"

—Art Williams

When you are "in the pits," everything is going wrong and your world seems to be falling apart - recruit!

Always remember:

A new recruit solves every problem in our business!

Field Training

"90% of your time should be spent field training."
—Art Williams

Field training is the most important thing that happens in your business.

Average Size Policy

"It is absolutely critical that we maintain an average size policy of $250,000 plus! This is important to MILICO profits, but even more importantly - that's what our clients need and deserve."
—Art Williams

A.L. Williams believes:

No. 1 - Never sell any kind of cash value life insurance.

A.L. Williams sells term 100% of the time ...

No. 2 - Never sell "2 separate policies" on husband and wife.

Always use the rider on the spouse ...

There are very few things that will get AN (RVP) NSD TERMINATED. THIS IS ONE OF THOSE THINGS.

A person who sells ONLY FOR COMMISSION without considering HIS CLIENT'S INTEREST is someone who is A TERRIBLE EMBARRASSMENT to the REAL A.L. Williams people and MUST BE ELIMINATED!

Steps to Winning

No. 1 - Identify your long-term goal

- 10 years- $90,000 income for life from your investments
- 1 year- RVP

No. 2 - Make a series of 90-day commitments

- 90 days - Become a Regional Manager
- 90 days - Double your monthly income

No. 3 - Reward yourself when you do well

If your income has been averaging $5,000 a month and you are paid $10,000 this month, celebrate and take your family or your spouse away for a weekend.

No. 4 - Punish yourself if you do badly

- Have a "Saturday practice"
- Start a recruiting blitz
- Start a policy pick-up blitz
- Double and triple your Asset Management presentations

Always Be Positive

"The single most important thing you can develop in your lifetime is a positive attitude."
Art Williams

No other trait - not experience, not knowledge - will produce as much for you as a positive, enthusiastic attitude. It can accomplish MIRACLES for you and your people.

No. 1 - 90+% of winning is always being excited. The key to staying excited: Always lead by example!

- Personally recruit
- Personally field train
- Make money and save money
- Work hard in the field
- Be the kind of person your people would like to become

No. 2 - Happy people attract others like them. Negative, frustrated people do, too.
No. 3 - Everyone loves to be around someone who is positive and excited about life. Negative people "drain your batteries."
No. 4 - A positive attitude is the key to staying motivated.

Most people stay motivated for two or three months. A few people stay motivated for two or three years. A winner stays motivated for as long as it takes to win.

No. 5 - You must practice a positive attitude.

A positive attitude doesn't happen overnight. It's OK to get down, discouraged and depressed - as long as you do it for a short time each day.

No. 6 - Pass negatives up and positives down.

- Talk to your up line if you're down and discouraged.
- Talk to your people when you're positive, excited and enthusiastic. Your bad attitude hurts your people's attitudes.

No. 7 - A leader helps promote a positive attitude among his people.

- Praise people for a positive attitude.
- Don't encourage people to complain. Don't let meetings turn into "gripe sessions."

No. 8 - A bad attitude is almost a guarantee of failure.

You can be smart, talented, good-looking and creative, but if you don't have the ability to be positive, you'll never make it.

Remember: always be positive!

No. 9 - Build a protective shell around you.

Everybody's going to worry, be disappointed, have problems. You must learn to protect yourself from hurts, not dwell on them. Let them pass and forget them. You must learn to "get tough" and steel your emotions, when necessary, against the bad things that happen to you and others. Your ability to deal with negatives or problems - and flush them out of your system and go on - determines whether or not you will be a success.

Get Your Priorities Straight

"You can't separate other areas of your life from your business life. A lousy family life, a lousy personal life, a lousy spiritual life will guarantee you a lousy business life."
—Art Williams

Great leaders know the importance of living a balanced life. At A.L. Williams, we believe that success in business is only a part of success in living. To be a happy, successful person, you must have all areas of your life in order.

No. 1 - Set Priorities.

We believe in God first, family second and A.L. Williams third.

No. 2 - Don't neglect your spiritual life.

Whatever your spiritual or religious beliefs, they can and do apply to your business life. Don't make the mistake of thinking that "anything goes" in business. The principles of decency and a moral life apply in business, too.

No. 3 - Learn to mix business with family life.

Most people tend to take their families for granted. Wrong! You must invest the time and energy it takes to have a happy marriage and family life, just like you do in business. Don't forget, that your family is who you're working so hard for in the first place.

No. 4 - Don't forget your "physical" well being.

Without good health, you won't be able to enjoy the success you're working so hard to achieve. Don't get too busy to eat right, exercise and care for your body. (I take time to exercise even when I'm on the road.)

Three Stages of Commitment

"Success at anything requires total commitment. You can't just 'sort of' commit; you can't commit three days a week. You must commit 110% to have a chance at winning."
—Art Williams

The first step to greatness is TOTAL COMMITMENT. Everyone goes through three stages before he has made "THE" TOTAL COMMITMENT.

No. 1 - Lying Stage

You can lie to everyone but yourself. At first, you go around telling everyone how committed you are and how great everything is. But deep inside, you are not really committed.

Finally, you get so tired of being average and ordinary, so tired of seeing everyone else get promotions and everyone else making money that you finally tell yourself "again" that "this is it." You tell yourself that you are REALLY COMMITTED, that you will "DO IT" THIS TIME.

No. 2 - Quitting Stage

Next, you begin to QUIT everytime you have a problem, miss a sale, lose a recruit, etc. You probably even go out and look for "a good job." But you CAN'T find any "good" jobs. So you RECOMMIT one more time ....

No. 3 - The "Do It" Stage

When you are so sick and tired of lying and quitting and being average and ordinary, when you finally make up your mind that you are through running, then you burn all your bridges and you know that A.L. Williams is it for you. You decide to be somebody or die trying ....

Then you take your "FIRST STEP TOWARD GREATNESS."

Desire Is the Key

"Don't pick your winners early. You can't measure their desire by a 'first impression.'"
—Art Williams

There is nothing sadder than to see a leader expect a person to succeed big because of looks, talent, education, experience, talk, etc. Most of the time those people turn out to be DUDS and recruits who look like duds because of their background turn out to BE STUDS.

Your responsibility as a leader is to put the 11 best players on the field.

- Don't pre-judge your people.
- Everyone starts out at the bottom.
- Everyone earns promotions by performance, not talk.

What do you look for in recruits?

- Desire
- Hunger to win

- Determination to "be somebody"

Most People Almost Do Enough to Win

"Most people can't stay motivated long enough to win."
—Art Williams

I have seen many people in A.L. Williams do "almost enough" to win. They fail to stay motivated long enough to do what it takes. People who can not stay motivated long enough usually have one or more of these four problems:

No. 1 - Don't really believe the dream can happen ...

You must think every day about how "great it will be to be financially independent ... (see yourself winning - dream every day.)

No. 2 - Don't have No. 1 priority of "helping people" ...

"Material things" and "money" alone won't give you the endurance, motivation and spirit necessary to "keep doing it."

No. 3 - Are not "crusaders" ...

Only by being a crusader will you have that "little extra amount of courage" necessary to win.

No. 4 - Fail to keep building or getting better ...

You can't wait for your people or your company to Do It for you. You "must" always "Do It " first. You "must" become "a better person."

You must WORK HARDER
You must BE MORE POSITIVE
You must BE MORE EXCITED
You must BE TOUGHER
You must BE MORE HONEST
You must BE MORE SINCERE
You must BE A BETTER SPOUSE

You must BE A BETTER PARENT
You must BE A BETTER PERSON

You Must Become a Dreamer Again

"If you want to be 'a winner,' you've got to become a 'dreamer' again."
—Art Williams

Most people in America have stopped dreaming. They grow up with everyone telling them how special they are. They are really "turned on" about life and about becoming somebody they'll be proud of... then they are thrown out in the "big, bad world," and companies and people start taking advantage of them.

These once enthusiastic people go into a shell.

They begin to develop an attitude that "life has passed me by - life has dealt me a bad hand!"

To win in life, I believe you must become a dreamer again. You must be excited, confident and turned on about life.

I dreamed every day for years about how great it

could feel to be financially independent. Those dreams kept me going when times were tough, but you know what I found out? Being financially independent was 100 TIMES GREATER than I dreamed it would be. No one can tell you how truly great it is being financially free unless he is there himself.

I don't know anyone who has become financially independent who hasn't paid a big price, but who doesn't look back and say, "It was worth it. If I had known how GREAT it would be, I would have been willing to pay a price 10 times greater."

One of the things I love about the United States and the free enterprise system is that you can become what you dream about. You can change! You can make it better for you and your family if you want to badly enough!

"Forbidden" Words

"As a leader, you set the tone and the mood for your people. In all your words and actions, remember that your people are looking to you to be an example."

—Art Williams

There is NO PLACE in A.L. Williams for:

No. 1 - I can't

You can not even consider the idea of failure. Instead, you must maintain an "EXPECTATION OF SUCCESS" for you and your people.

No. 2 - My

It should always be "you," "we" and "our." A selfish attitude will destroy even the most motivated team. Put "the team" before yourself.

Time

"Time is the greatest single investment you can make in your business."
—Art Williams

I believe that you CAN'T FAIL in A.L. Williams if you're willing to SPEND TIME on your business.

No. 1 - Spend time learning the business
No. 2 - Spend time prospecting
No. 3 - Spend time recruiting
No. 4 - Spend time field training
No. 5 - Spend time getting referrals
No. 6 - Spend time building personal relationships

Remember: Winning doesn't take brilliance, a college education or a privileged background. Winning just takes time.

The "Little" Things Make "the Difference"

"Most leaders are always trying to hit a 'home run' - make the big sale, recruit the giant, wrong again! The key to winning in A.L. Williams is doing the 'little things' right."

—Art Williams

Most leaders worry the most about the "big decisions" they must make in their careers. I've always found that the big decisions are often the easiest, and usually have an obvious solution.

In business, it's the "little, day-to-day" decisions that are tough. Ultimately, it's your day-to-day actions that will determine whether you succeed or fail.

Learn how to do the "little things" right, and the big things will take care of themselves.

Some tips ...

No. 1 - The toughest management decisions are the every day decisions

---

These are also the most important.

- When it's time for work, deciding whether to get up and go or stay in bed
- When you lose a sale, deciding to go out and pick up another set of policies
- When your best person quits, deciding to go out and immediately recruit someone to take his place

---

No. 2 - Leaders learn to follow their instincts.

You can't always call your upline or call the home office whenever you have a problem. You must trust yourself and your ability to make decisions.

No. 3 - Learn from your mistakes.

Experience is the greatest teacher in the world. You learn by screwing up. If you worry about making mistakes, you will make more mistakes. BE AGGRESSIVE!

No. 4 - You don't win with "tricks and gimmicks."

You win with FUNDAMENTALS ("blocking and tackling"- prospecting, field training, and recruiting).

You win by committing to "a system" (not changing every time you get to a meeting).

No. 5 - Remember: This is an "endurance contest" - not a "sprint."

Victory will go to those who "want to" the MOST, and "keep fighting" the LONGEST.

Always Be Excited

"90+% of winning is always being excited ... especially when you don't feel like being excited."
—Art Williams

Don't Feel Guilty

"The greatest thing you can do for your people is for you to win and prove that paying that 'nasty price' was worth it."
—Art Williams

One of the biggest problems facing an RVP that begins to have great financial success is GUILT. This is because MOST of the people in his organization will always be PAYING THE PRICE and struggling financially (YOU had to pay the price, too).

You have two primary responsibilities to your people:

No. 1 - Give them an opportunity that is real and be there to deliver for them.
No. 2 - Prove that the opportunity is real by winning. You make big money, save big money and earn big promotions.

Remember: You can't "do it" for your people; everyone must pay his price, but you can prove to them that it's worth it.

Avoid Panic Management

"If you are ever forced to make a management decision based on how it affects you, you will never be a great leader!"
—Art Williams

There are 3 areas that cause you to make panic management decisions:

No. 1 - Poor personal financial position ...

Never make a decision when one of your considerations is how it affects your income.

You must be liquid, keep expenses low and save, save, save ....

No. 2 - Too little activity ...

This is a numbers business. Always work to increase activity- number of recruits, number of policy pick-ups, number of presentations, number of legs, number of RVPs, etc.

No. 3 - No definite management philosophy ...

You win by consistently doing the right things long enough. You can't change directions every time you meet a disappointment.

Charge!

"A good leader keeps moving, regardless of whether times are good or bad."
—Art Williams

The sales business is a business of "momentum." A leader's job is to keep that momentum going. As any great leader - or any football coach - will tell you, once you lose momentum, it's three times harder to get it back again.

I believe the answer is to "keep charging" forward.

CHARGE! - when things are going great
CHARGE! - when momentum begins to slow down
CHARGE! - when you feel good
CHARGE! - when you don't feel like it
CHARGE! - every single day, regardless of the circumstances - and keep charging until you win!

How to "keep charging":

No. 1 - Keep activity up.

- Everyone in your organization should be doing something all the time (meeting a prospect for lunch, visiting a client's home, selling, recruiting, etc.). Respond to problems by "picking up" activity even more.

Example:

1. You receive a chargeback ...
   CHARGE - go out and make another sale.
2. Your best recruit quits ...
   CHARGE - go out and recruit three new people.
3. Your prospect doesn't buy ...
   CHARGE - go out and pick up another policy.

No. 2 - Get mad.

- Get mad about some "wrong" or "injustice" and go fight it. It's hard to "charge" if you don't much care about what you're doing.
- Don't be discouraged. See problems as opportunities for growth.

No. 3 - Believe in yourself.

- Believe you can achieve your goals.

- Read THINK AND GROW RICH by Napoleon Hill for a description of the "common denominators" to success. Follow his "6-step plan."

No. 4 - Know where you're going.

- Set DEFINITE goals and a plan for achieving them.
- Involve your family in your goal-setting.
- Don't be afraid to "dream." That's the FUEL for your goals.

No. 5 - Don't accept anything but success.

- Commit to doing "whatever it takes" to reach your goals.
- Realize that every great reward has a great price.
- Develop persistence. "Keep on keeping on" no matter what happens.
- Never give up.

Expect to Win

"If you think you can or if you think you can't, you're right."
—Art Williams

Most people have been so hurt, so taken advantage of, so put down, that they don't like themselves anymore.

They have developed an attitude that:

- "I don't care how great the opportunity is, I'll find a way to screw it up. I have screwed up everything else I've touched .... "
- "I don't care how great a person you say my RVP is, he'll find a way to screw me.
  — Everyone always has .... "
  — Life will eventually turn out for you the way you see it turning out.
- You must see good things happening.
- You must like yourself again.
- You must be excited about life again.

You Must Pay A Price

"Nothing worth having comes easy. People must recognize the fact that big dreams have big prices, and determine the price they're willing to pay for success."
—Art Williams

Only a small percentage of people are willing to "pay the price" that's required for great success. Here are some important points to remember:

No. 1 - The harder you work, the luckier you get

Isn't it funny how the "lucky people" are always the hardest workers? There's no substitute for hard work.

No. 2 - Sacrifice

Learn to do without things if doing so will get you closer to your goal. Practice self-discipline.

No. 3 - The greater the reward, the greater the price

If your goal is to make extra income for your family, then you will not have much trouble reaching it. If your goal is NSD, be prepared to pay a great price.

No. 4 - Winning is better than you ever dreamed

Any successful person who has "made it" will tell you that success is better than he ever dreamed.

No. 5 - Build confidence and staying power

Paying a price has benefits! It builds your ability to do something well and your mental attitude. If you've learned to pay a price, you will know that you can take whatever they throw at you.

Think Big – Don't Major in Minor Things

"Always remember that you only make money when you make a sale. The most important thing that happens in A.L. Williams takes place across the kitchen table with the husband and wife."
—Art Williams

Various kinds of meetings and other activities are important. But remember ...

You don't make money at:

- Meetings
- Training classes
- Fast Start Schools

And, you don't make money:

- Doing paperwork
- Reading commission statements
- Studying for your securities license

- Attending RVP meetings
- Attending SVP meetings
- Going to conventions

You do make money:

Across the kitchen table with a husband and wife talking about recruiting, the evils of cash value insurance, the theory of decreasing responsibility, and how to save clients money.

How can you make sure you're majoring in "major" things?

The key: Always look at yourself as a DISTRICT LEADER.

If you always do the things you did as a District Leader, you will never stop growing.

For example:

Be everything to everybody.
Field train four nights a week.
Give two presentations per night.
Make one personal recruit every week.

Remember ...

Until you consistently cash flow $12,000 to $16,000 a month, you should never depend on overrides. You make your money PERSONALLY and treat OVERRIDES AS A BONUS.

Surge

"When activity levels off, it's up to the leader to 'make things happen'."
—Art Williams

One of the most frustrating things about building an organization is that sales and income don't go up consistently every single month. Remember: this is a business of MOMENTUM.

I believe in two rules when you think of momentum:

No. 1 - When you have momentum, get all you can get.

- Recruits
- Sales
- Income, etc.

No. 2 - When you lose momentum, Blitz.

- Policy pick-up contests
- Recruiting contests
- Double and triple activity.

Always remember: If your activity and momentum have leveled off, all you need are "one or two good recruits or clients" to get a new surge.

The Magic of "90 Days"

"You can do anything for 90 days."
—Art Williams

There are two types of goals:

No. 1 - Long-Term Goals

These are always your FIRST GOALS. For example: financial independence or becoming an RVP. These are the goals that give you direction and motivation.

No. 2 - Short-Term Goals

It normally takes a long time to accomplish your long-term goals and it's tough to stay motivated for one year or five years or even ten years.

But you can do anything for 90 days.

Setting short-term goals, like 90-day goals, gives you a "sense of urgency" and day-today motivation to keep moving toward your big goals.

I built my entire career on a series of 90-day commitments. I believe you can CHANGE YOUR LIFE in 90 days. Most people stay at something ALMOST LONG ENOUGH, but they STOP LONG ENOUGH to LOSE all their MOMENTUM. If you work like mad for 90 days, you will reach a NEW HIGH in your business life. This new high will give you the CONFIDENCE and COURAGE to "Go For It" again and again until you WIN!

Work like "mad" for 90 days.

Don't get "too high" or "too low."

Things are "never" as good or as bad as they seem at the moment.

Don't "stop" for any reason.

"Review" your results only after 90 days. (You can't look at management on a day-by-day basis. Management results come after weeks of paying the price. You grow out of periods of plateaus.)

At the end of 90 days, "recommit" for another 90 days with new and greater goals or "get out" of this business.

Reward and Punish

In order to reach your goals, you need to reward yourself when you do good and punish yourself when you do badly.

A Personal Example

The program of goal setting I used when I was coaching football is an example of the process above.

Long-term goal: Becoming state champions

Short-term goal: Improving with every game until the team became state champions

If we WON and had a GREAT game ...

Great offensively - win by more than 21 points ...

Great defensively - win and defense held opponent to no points ...

We REWARDED ourselves with a short practice with no pads on Monday.

If we WON but DIDN'T HAVE A GREAT GAME ...

Won, but not by 21 points OR

Won, but other team scored

We PUNISHED ourselves with a long practice with pads on Monday.

If we GOT BEAT ...

We ADDED A DAY and had full practice on SATURDAY.

Hang Tough

"The challenge of any leader is to not let the losers, the disappointments, the pressure, the competition and the rejection change you and make you negative and bitter."

—Art Williams

You must stay excited and enthusiastic. Negative people make others feel bad.

People can't stand to be around these kind of people. You must show excitement - especially when you don't feel like being excited.

No. 1 - You must develop a mental toughness.

Just like you can't quit when a prospect says no, you can't quit being excited, positive and happy when someone or something disappoints you.

No. 2 - Live for your good people.

Don't take things personally. Always remember that 99% of your people are good, honest and appreciate you in A.L. Williams. Don't let that 1% make you a bad leader for the other 99%.

No. 3 - Play a game.

The bigger you get, the more pressure, problems, rejection and challenges you will have. Play a game with yourself. See how much you can take and still be positive.

The Magic of "Working Hard"

"Work every day as if your career depended on it. It does!"
—Art Williams

Many geniuses die broke. Many talented people never accomplish anything.

But ...

many average, ordinary people BEAT all the rest.

Why?

Because they're willing to WORK HARDER than anyone else.

Remember ...

- You can beat 50% of the people JUST BY WORKING HARD. (Most people won't work hard enough or long enough to win.)
- You can beat another 40% by LIVING RIGHT.
- The top 10% is a DOGFIGHT in the free enterprise system.

Don't Let Fear Stop You!

"99% of the things you fear never happen. Don't waste time worrying about what might go wrong."

—Art Williams

Some people let fear totally destroy them in business. Fear holds more people back than lack of opportunity or talent. It's important to remember that winning big means taking chances - and not letting fear get hold of your life.

No. 1 - Don't fear things you can't control!

The best way to stop worrying: learn to trust your instincts. Do what you think is best at the time, then don't worry about it. You can't agonize over every decision.

All you can control is your attitude and your activity.

No. 2 - Don't fear what other people will say!

Keep your goals in front of you and believe in yourself. Don't let other people's opinions shape your goals and your future. Don't worry about controversy. People don't like change and they sometimes react badly to new things. Remember: every great movement in business and industry has been controversial. Just be proud to be a part of something great and refuse to be discouraged.

No. 3 - Don't fear the competition

Don't worry about whether other people are doing better than you, or whether you're progressing fast enough. If you give it all you've got, keep getting better and are willing to do whatever it takes to win, you'll be OK. Being envious or jealous of others around you will only take your focus away from you and your business.

Give it your best and if that's not enough- so what! You don't score a touchdown on every play. ALWAYS keep fighting!

Remember: all you can do is all you can do; but all you can do is enough!

Impatient for Success

"One characteristic that I've observed about every great leader I've known is that they're never satisfied. They always want to do more, accomplish more, become more. They're always impatient for success."

—Art Williams

The real winners in business - and in life - are the people who always want more.

For them, things never happen fast enough. There just aren't enough hours in the day for them to do all the things they want to do.

Winners are never patient. They know what they want to do, and they can't rest 'til they "do it."

Characteristics of winners

- They're maniacs!

They have a dream, and they "live, sleep and eat" their dream until they win.

- They're nuts!

They'll do whatever it takes to win - work 20 hours a day, seven days a week, have three "lunch" appointments a day with prospects - anything that gets them further toward their goal.

- They're emotional!

They get EXCITED about their job, they get MAD at the competition, they get TOTALLY INVOLVED with their people.

- They won't be denied!

They never let the negatives, the frustrations and the disappointments get them down. They don't worry, hurt or cry for very long. They refuse to accept anything but success.

They're impatient to win. .. and they always do!

A Little Bit More

"To win, you must do everything you are supposed to, and 'a little bit more.'"
—Art Williams

A.L. Williams had two RVPs in Dallas, Texas in 1984. One RVP was paid over $500,000 and the other was paid $50,000.

What was the difference?

- On the surface, everything seemed THE SAME -
  - — same age

- same sex
- same position
- same products
- same city
- same training
- same company
- same state
- same benefits

• Also, both did everything you should do to win -

- worked hard
- sacrificed
- loyal to A.L. Williams
- treated people "good"
- good recruiting
- good training
- good administration
- good in every area

But why did one earn $500,000 and the other earn $50,000?

The $500,000 RVP did everything you are supposed to do, and "a little bit more."

He:

- sacrificed and a little bit more
- worked hard and a Little bit more

— was loyal to A.L. Williams and a little bit more
— treated people "good" and a little bit more
— was a good recruiter and a little bit more
— made money and a little bit more
— saved money and a little bit more

Always Play Scared

"Every great person wakes up every day scared his business will fail. Fear of failure is one of the key motivators for outstanding business success."
—Art Williams

- Wake up thinking the bubble will burst.
- Never take for granted your success.
- Anticipate and expect difficulties.
- Be always "playing scared," you'll be more prepared for any problems that do come.
- Work feeling that you always need one more sale because you think you'll lose one and get a chargeback.

- Always SAVE more money - because your business might go under.
- Always wait on signing a lease, buying a typewriter, expanding your office or hiring an additional secretary.
- Always hold off buying a new home, car or personal things for fear you'll have a business reversal.
- Be cautious. Be prepared for the worst so that if it happens, you'll be ready and it won't cause you to fail or give up.

Basic guidelines:

- Don't ever expand your business until 90 days after you feel a need. Make sure your momentum is for real.
- Don't change your personal standard of living for two years after you've reached a new plateau of success.
- Prepare for the worst, the unexpected and you'll not be overcome by it.

Work Two or More Levels Below You

"You make money in the field, not in the office."
—Art Williams

It is critically important that you understand that 90+% of your time should be spent field training.

In our business, you "continue to grow or you begin to die." You continue to grow by always recruiting and always making promotions (Remember: Keep 'em coming and going).

You MUST also understand "SPREAD." You MUST work 2 or more levels below you for two reasons:

No. 1 - You are paid to build leaders.

When you build a district leader, you must go out and build another district leader.

(You must have 3 to 5 direct recruits to you at all times.)

No. 2 - It is the only way you can survive financially until you have produced 7 to 10 first generation RVPs.

Example: Base Shop Spread

RVP Advances= $60.01 -Override from a sale of a regional manager's organization.

RVP Advances= $412.14- Override from an RVP, field trainee and new recruit.

"Based On: Average advance on typical sale of Common Sense Term Policy.

Excuses Don't Count

"Excuses are the 'easy way out.'"
—Art Williams

Everyone has a convenient excuse not to act.

- "I don't have any money."
- "I don't have any time."

- "I'll do it tomorrow."
- "People like me don't have a chance."
- "I can't change after all these years."

Excuses don't count.

Everyone has the ability to begin RIGHT NOW to take control of his life.

Everyone can begin today to follow a plan that will lead to success and financial independence.

You can do it!

Remember: Excuses don't count in the big leagues!

Fight

"Life will give you whatever you're willing to fight for."
—Art Williams

I used to tell my football players that if they thought those guys in the "wrong colored" jerseys were going to "roll over and play dead" and give them the game, they were dead wrong.

The other team was going to try to knock their heads off!

If you want to win, you'd better PUT YOUR UNIFORM ON and be ready to FIGHT!

I believe that life will give you what you will fight for. It's not enough to just want to win.

- If you will "take" being average and ordinary, life will give you that.
- If you will accept being poor, life will make you poor.
- If you will accept being unhappy, life will make you unhappy.
- If you want to win, you must ROLL OUT OF THE BED, PUT YOUR UNIFORM ON - and FIGHT!

Always Be Willing to Start Over

"You never lose unless you stop trying."
—Art Williams

One of my "theories" about winning at A.L. Williams is this: "YOUR FIRST 18 MONTHS, EVERYTHING YOU DO TURNS TO CRAP."

No. 1 - Don't expect things to be easy

So many people fail because they think that just because we have a fabulous product, fabulous part-time opportunity and a tremendous competitive advantage, that every client should buy and every recruit should "make it."

It just doesn't work that way.

No. 2 - Winners never quit

Winners know that they are going to have problems and disappointments, so whenever they hurt and want to quit - just like everyone else - they CAN'T QUIT.

They just won't let themselves. They pick up, start over and do it one more time.

All You Can Do Is All You Can Do

"Don't worry about things you can't control. If you fail, pick yourself up and try it 'one more time.'"
—Art Williams

In a football game, of say, 120 plays, only one or two plays go a LONG way for a TOUCHDOWN. 95% of the plays DON'T WORK like you had planned.

The team that wins:

- Believes every play will score a touchdown.
- Keeps calling another play, another play, another play, and another play until they win.

In our business, when you do EVERYTHING YOU POSSIBLY CAN (sell the best product, offer the best opportunity, etc.) and one thing doesn't work just right, CALL ANOTHER PLAY!

All you can do is all you can do.

LEADERSHIP RESPONSIBILITIES

IN THIS SECTION:

- Freedom with Responsibility
- ALW Freedoms
- ALW Responsibilities
- Build Crusaders
- Capacity to Win .
- Provide Positive Leadership
- Leadership is Everything
- Build Personal Relationships
- Manage Activity, Not Sales
- Saving Money
- Your "Team" Responsibility
- Sales Requirements
- Controlled Growth
- Successful Recruiting .
- Protected Client and Protected Recruit
- The "Worst Hurt"
- How to Always Stay Motivated

Freedom with Responsibility

"The 'freedom with responsibility' concept is the essence of the free enterprise system and one of the most cherished principles in A.L. Williams."
—Art Williams

There is a serious disease going around the United States called "The 'GIMME' ILLNESS!" It seems that far too many Americans think only about, "WHAT EVERYONE SHOULD DO FOR 'ME'! "

"GIMME" MY FREEDOM
"GIMME" MY RIGHTS
"GIMME" MORE MONEY
"GIMME" MY PROMOTION

These people never think about their responsibility.

Remember: There can never be freedom without responsibility.

ALW Freedoms

A.L. Williams believes in giving its people TREMENDOUS FREEDOM ... the freedom to:

No. 1 - Always do more.

- Always earn more
- Always sell more
- Always recruit more
- Build it as big as you want
- Use the entire ALW and MILICO support systems

No. 2 - As an RVP, operate with unlimited territories.

- See 150-mile rule

No. 3 - Be your own boss.

- Manage your own expenses and activity
- Choose the career path that's right for you (part-time income or full-time career)
- Use the entire ALW and MILICO support system

No. 4 - Become totally financially independent.

ALW Responsibilities

A.L. Williams believes that every person has a RESPONSIBILITY to PROTECT our company and to GIVE SOMETHING BACK to our company ... you have a responsibility to:

- Never jeopardize the future of our company and our people ... protect and support the team
- Never take advantage of your people
- Always do what's best for the consumer
- Don't violate A.L. Williams' principles and traditions

- Provide positive leadership ... be a winning example
- Keep working ... RVPs, SVPs and NSDs can't "retire on the job"
- Recruit and sell in the right market
- Wake up every day and do something to HELP your people and your company GET BETTER.

Build Crusaders

"The first step to building a winning team is building crusaders."
—Art Williams

How to build crusaders

No. 1 - Sell the A.L. Williams concept first.
No. 2 - Show the "wrong" done by the traditional industry and the cash value concept.
No. 3 - Show people the good they can do in A.L. Williams.

- Help people save money
- Help people get more value for the money they spend
- Provide death protection for families in case of the loss of the breadwinner
- Provide opportunity for financial security
- Offer the greatest business opportunity in America

Why you should build crusaders

Two reasons ...

No. 1 - Crusaders are the glue that holds your team together.

No. 2 - A crusading spirit gives people the courage they need to win.

Crusading spirit inspires activity:

Crusaders "die hard"

Crusading spirit gives motivation and courage to keep going when times get tough

Everyone wants to commit to something "bigger" than just his business. (Nobody wants to just make a living.)

Be an example of the crusading spirit.

Give people an example of commitment to "doing what's right"

Show people your own devotion and belief

Show people that A.L. Williams isn't just another job

Create involvement in the crusade

Provide inspiration and leadership

Capacity to Win

"In order to become truly successful, you must develop the capacity to always get better."
—Art Williams

At one time in my career, I believed in "the Peter Principle," that people will eventually rise to their level of incompetence. I saw a number of people reach a certain level of success and then "level off" or even go backwards. I saw others who continued to get better. Now, I believe I know why.

As A LEADER, I believe you must develop the capacity to GET BETIER in EIGHT MAJOR AREAS:

No. 1 - The capacity to be happy

- Do what's necessary to "feel good" about yourself.

Stay in good physical shape (keep your weight down, take care of yourself). Maintain good appearance. Always look neat, clean and professional. You'll feel good about yourself, and that good feeling will affect those around you.

- Take a look at the GOOD THINGS in your life.

It's amazing how most people seem to dwell on the things in their life that aren't perfect. Look at the good things you have going for you - your family, a growing business, your health.

No. 2 - The capacity to be excited about your job

It's true that "the grass always looks greener on the other side." It's easy to be excited about someone else's job. The challenge is to be excited about your own.

Whether you're a rep, RVP, or NSD, stop looking at

what other people have accomplished and concentrate on doing the best you can possibly do, WHERE YOU ARE RIGHT NOW. If you do that, you'll be SURE TO get to the top.

No. 3 - The capacity to always get better

Never be satisfied with your accomplishments. Get up each day determined to make it a "better day" than the one before. Make every presentation better, make every Fast Start School better, have a better family life, a better business life. Make "getting better" a short-range goal that you check EVERY DAY!

No. 4 - The capacity to "compete"

- You can't just go out there and stand on the playing field. You must COMPETE in order to win.
- You must "pay the price" for success. Life is a balance sheet - for everything you get you have to make sacrifices.
- Every winner wants to quit and go home every day - but he doesn't!
- People who work the hardest accomplish the most.

- Remember: The harder you work, the "luckier" you get.

No. 5 - The capacity to "survive" success

- Don't let success change you.
  - Keep doing the things that made you successful.
  - Continue to develop your personal strengths.
  - Don't get caught in the "management trap" - sitting in a big office, doing only"administrative" work.
- Don't get "too good" to do the little things.
- Remember: No job is too small for a great leader.
- Don't forget about your people. They helped you get where you are.

No. 6 - The capacity to "dream big"

- Set your heart on something.
- Have a goal of GREATNESS. Don't settle for just doing "a little."

No. 7 - The capacity to grow as a person

- Your people see you "first" as a person.
- Keep improving your business, family and spiritual life.
- Strive to be right - morally and ethically 100% of the time.
- Remember: Before you can become a great leader, you've got to become a great person.

No. 8 - The capacity to "win"

- Winning builds mental attitude and expectation of success.
- Once you start winning, you can't stop!
- Winning is BETTER than you ever imagined.

Provide Positive Leadership

"At A.L. Williams, we believe in leadership vs. 'management.' Managers manage things. Leaders lead people."
—Art Williams

We believe that our system of management puts the human touch back into the business world and helps people achieve their maximum potential in business and in life.

AL W Leaders...
Care about people

- They build strong personal relationships
- They stand by their people through good times and bad
- They treat people with respect

AL W Leaders...
Motivate and lead

- They deal with people "one-on-one"
- They are accessible - never too busy for their people
- They motivate, but never intimidate
- They look for people's strengths and ignore weakness
- They always have a positive attitude
- They always "do it" first
- They stay excited and enthusiastic about the business
- They push up their people

AL W Leaders ...
Do what's right

- They are honest, sincere and loyal
- They live by their word
- They put the good of the team above self
- They are an example of a "balanced life"
- They are crusaders
- They have beliefs and stand for something
- They don't run from problems
- They have a total commitment to their people and their business
- They dream big and expect to succeed

- They never ask their people to do anything they haven't done

ALW Leaders
NEVER GIVE UP

Leadership Is Everything

"It is no accident that your people make money, your quality of business is excellent, and you build a business that will give your family financial independence. Leaders make things happen."
—Art Williams

This business takes hard work, planning, and leadership.

To be successful, you must do the right things on the front end.

You must:

No. 1 - Recruit the right market.
No. 2 - Sell the right market.

No. 3 - Sell the right product.
No. 4 - Sell the product right.
No. 5 - Train your people to "do it" right.
No. 6 - Check up and make sure it's done right.

Danger Areas:

- Leaders "not" trained properly
- New recruits not receiving "enough training and attention"
- "New insurance sales," no replacement
- "Young, single" men and women
- More than one application per family
- New recruits not observing "a minimum of three field training sales"
- New recruit's personal sales not going through "the three-step sales process"
- New rep, manager, or RVP making "an unusually large number of sales" in a short time
- Low income "families"
- "Unemployed"
- "Low face amounts" on spouse
- More than an occasional "not-taken policy"
- Sales by "former insurance salespeople"
- Sales on "1st interview" (against company policy)

Build Personal Relationships

"People don't care how much you know, until they know how much you care."
—Art Williams

You must get to know your people and let them know you care about them and their families.

No. 1 - Get to know your people on a first-name basis, including their spouses and families.
No. 2 - Invite your people to your house, a picnic, ballgame or other special event.
No. 3 - Remember: you work for your people - your people don't work for you.
No. 4 - Show your people that you care about them and their success.
No. 5 - Make an "unconditional commitment" to your people - live with them through good times and bad times.
No. 6 - Look for people's good qualities and praise them.

No. 7 - Make each person in your organization feel special:

- Master the art of recognition
- Stay in constant contact with your people

No. 8 - Be slow to criticize.
No. 9 - Always be positive and excited about their future.
No. 10 - Always "sell the dream."

BUILDING PRINCIPLE: You get paid to build successful people, not sales.

Manage Activity, Not Sales

"Sales and income are the result of 'doing things right' on the front end."
—Art Williams

You win by doing "the right thing" on the front end. You must first pick up policies, make the presentation, hire a new recruit, etc. before you worry about anything else.

Never worry about making money. If you manage activity, your income will follow automatically.

Why is managing activity so important? Because this business is, and always will be, a NUMBERS BUSINESS.

Those who see the most people make the most money.

- Remember: You make money IN THE FIELD, not in the office.
- The leader must "do it first." If you want your people to recruit, YOU must recruit.

That's true in every area of the business. Always LEAD BY EXAMPLE!

- When you get the momentum, GET ALL YOU CAN GET!
  (You can never recruit too many good people.)
- Always do "a little bit more" - one more presentation, one more recruit. one more policy pick-up, etc.

Weekly field training activity goal for full-time people

- Two presentations a night - four nights a week
- One new recruit per week
- Three policy pick-ups per week

Monitor activity

Keep a list of the following on all full-timers and keep it posted in the office:

- Number of recruits
- Number of presentations (across the kitchen table)
- Number of policy pick-ups

Activity blitz

Have an activity blitz when your momentum begins to slow down ...

Recruiting blitz

Policy pick-up blitz

ACTIVI1Y BLITZ motivates and excites people to do a "little bit more" - gives a new MOMENTUM to your organization.

ACTIVI1Y PRINCIPLE: If you ever need one thing to work for you - one sale, one recruit, one leader, etc.

-you will always lose. You must have "the Law of Large Numbers" in your favor.

Saving Money

"Cash flows of our leaders are fantastic! One of your major responsibilities to your family, your people and your company is managing your cash flow and saving money."
—Art Williams

A.L. Williams is here forever and will continue to be a growing success. Individual RVPs must be prepared for the peaks and valleys their region will experience. The first month you earn $10,000 will not likely be a continually repeated event for a while. Be prepared financially for the set -backs, the interim lean times before your big income becomes secure big income over a period of time.

You must SAVE BIG MONEY and prepare for two things:

No. 1 - The possibility of "set-backs" and "emergencies ..."
No. 2 - To build "total financial independence" for your family ...

I will not accept an A.L. Williams RVP being paid big money and blowing it.

I believe an RVP that can't manage his or her money is just as "big-a-dud" as an RVP that cries all the time and can't make any money!

Your "Team" Responsibility

"As a leader or RVP in A.L. Williams you have a responsibility to protect our company."
—Art Williams

You "must" never take advantage of your position You "must" never use people for your own personal gain ... You "must" never do anything illegal or unethical that could endanger AL Williams.

Your team responsibility

- Team more important than any individual!
  - Never mishandle the money paid to you or your people!
- Manage and train in the legal way and the right way to sell!
  - Train to sell the right way 100% of the time!
  - Check and make sure it is done right!
  - Have meetings to remind your people of their responsibilities!
- Great quality of business is the difference in success and failure!
  - Not takens - Maximum of 20%!
  - Persistency- Minimum of 75%
- Control system to catch potential problems!
  - Do not run away from problems!
  - Turn negatives into positives.

Sale Requirements

"You have a responsibility as a leader in A.L. Williams to make money. You have a responsibility to your people to win."
—Art Williams

You must never let your people down. As an RVP or SVP, you are ALWAYS a leader.

It is IMPOSSIBLE TO HAVE long range success without maintaining a strong base shop.

Base shop minimum production requirements:**

All reps must produce one sale every six months.***

All qualified RVPs and SVPs must produce a minimum of three sales and $1,200 in submitted premium during any 30 day period or six sales and $2,400 submitted premium during any 60-day period to remain an RVP.

** Subject to change. Contract regulations~ control.

*** Subject to change

Controlled Growth

"The key to long range success is controlled growth! It is tough to manage explosive growth, but it can be done very effectively."
—Art Williams

The following are areas of POTENTIAL CONCERN in a FAST GROWING ORGANIZATION:

No. 1 - When a new Rep, Manager, or organization "explodes," you must personally go inspect eyeball-to- eyeball ...
No. 2 - You must follow the A.L. Williams Guidelines "exclusively ..."
No. 3 - Recruit A.L. Williams type people - use The A.L. Williams Profile (25 and up, married, children, employed with minimum income of $30,000, etc.) ...
No. 4 - You must not sell on the first interview. A policy should never be picked up without a full presentation and a good commitment from the prospect ...

No. 5 - Each new recruit must observe a minimum of three field training sales before he is allowed to make a sale ...
No. 6 - You must use the A.L. Williams Asset Management Presentation exclusively ...
No. 7 - You must recruit people "one-on-one." Client Night meetings are to show the "bigness" of A.L. Williams and reinforce the opportunity.
No. 8 - Every personal sale must be made "one-on-one" across the kitchen table" - never in groups or at meetings ...
No. 9 - Fundamentals - Always preach, teach and review fundamentals. Build successful leaders in getting referrals, strong commitment, closing sales, prospecting, great presentation, etc.
No. 10 - Build strong personal relationships- You and your leaders get to know all your people. Really care about your people. Spend time with your people.

A.L. Williams has had too many organizations that were "not making money" and "not making progress." Most of these organizations were working hard, but working dumb. They were seeing large numbers, getting large numbers to client night meetings, turning in large numbers of hiring papers, but not having any real success. The reason for this, I believe, was the following:

- Leaders were weak fundamentally ....
- Poor quality of recruits ....
- Not spending enough time with prospects, clients, and recruits ....

I believe this is a numbers business. I know, however, that "long range success" goes to those who "do it right" and always remain fundamentally strong!

Successful Recruiting

"Recruiting must become a state of mind."
—Art Williams

No. 1 - Recruiting law

- Hire selective masses
- Identify winners and challenge them
- The only way to hire quality is to hire quantity.

No. 2 - You must develop a recruiting philosophy

- Recruiting - an all-the-time thing
- Recruiting - a state-of-the-mind

Sub-rules

- Slow down in recruiting - Increase activity
- When you have momentum - Get all you can get
- Best way to recruit - Through your people (referrals)
- Be innovative - Try different methods of prospecting
- Have a plan for talented reps
- Consistency - Recruit 24 hours a day

The best rules to follow

- Best "recruit" - Crusader first.
- Best "referral"- From a new recruit.

- Best way to "prospect for recruits" - By selling the opportunity.
- Best "prospect" - Greenies.
- Best way to keep "a positive attitude" in organization- (Keep 'em coming and going).
- Best 'way to maintain "good momentum" - (Work 2 or more levels below you).
- Best "leaders" - A personal winning example (You - always be hardest worker and the No. 1 recruiter).
- Best attitude of leaders- You always "do it" first!
- Best "plan" for "good cash flow" - Until your cash flow is $12,000 to $18,000 per month, don't count on overrides - Live off your personal activity.
- Best "game plan" -
  - Recruit
  - Field train
- Best "goals" -
  - Full-time manager recruit a minimum of 1 new recruit per week.
  - Full-time manager average 1 sale per day (insurance or securities).
  - You average a minimum of 5 to 10 new referrals per sale; Average 20 to 25 new referrals per recruit.

  - Get new recruit in the field within 72 hours.
  - You get minimum of 6-8 PPU's and/or CNA's per new recruit.
  - You get minimum of 3 field training sales must be observed by each new recruit.
  - You get 4 to 5 recruits for new recruit's organization from each new recruit's natural market.
- Best way to "build strong personal relationships" - (Believe in your people through good times and bad times).
- Best "recruiting philosophy" - Only way to hire quality is to hire quantity.
- Best "market" - Middle America.
- Best teams "avoid":
  - New Reps who would sell to low income market.
  - New reps who would sell to young market.
  - New reps who live more than 50 miles from the office.
  - New reps who have insurance license.
  - New reps who have poor personal financial situation.
- Best "attitude" - Be positive all the time.
- Best "concept"- Work with those who deserve it, not need it.

- Best "organization"-A lot doing a little bit, but a few doing a lot.
- Best way to keep a "winning spirit" - Get all of your new recruits, prospects, and clients to a client night, investment seminar, or a Fast Start to see the bigness of AL Williams.
- Best way to "fail" - Recruit only winners, be selective, or recruit small numbers.
- Best thing to tell your "RVP trainees" - Recruit 75 to 100 people to become an RVP.
- Best "advice" for those who want to make it big - You can't recruit too many of the right kind of people.
- Best way to make promotions - Try not to pick your winners too early, and let production, not talk, be your guide.
- Best "asset" needed for new recruit to be great - Tremendous desire to be somebody.
- Best way to "kill recruiting" - Let the negative people, non-producers and losers change you and make you negative.
- Best way to "see income go down" - Have too many meetings - You make money and learn this business in the field.
- Best "recruiting organizations" - Always make the most money.

- Best "reason" to recruit - Only way to build a secure income and an unlimited income. Salespeople are unemployed every day.
- Best way to keep your people "motivated" - Always sell "The Dream."
- Best way to maintain "people's success" - Check their recruiting activity each week.
- Best recruiting "time frame" - 90 day commitment.

Protected Client and Protected Recruit

"It is your responsibility to win, but not at the expense of others. You have a responsibility to do what's right, first."
—Art Williams

Mandatory rules:

No. 1 - Protected Client ...

Once an A.L. Williams person has picked up a set of policies, that prospect is protected for 30 days ... If you contact this prospect, you should ENCOURAGE him to buy from the A.L. Williams person who got there FIRST.

No. 2 - Protected recruit

Once a recruit has submitted a complete set of hiring papers (check, all papers, etc.) that recruit belongs to that RVP's organization ...

(The SPOUSE of a recruit must work [if she/he chooses to get licensed] with THE SAME RVP.)

The "Worst Hurt"

"It is important that you build it right 'the first time.'"
—Art Williams

I want to bring to your attention a potential "DEVASTATING PROBLEM":

98% of the people are UNABLE TO PAY THE PRICE

to build an organization that will produce them a big income. The "WORST HURT" to me in this business is to see a leader, new rep or RVP finally get his business going great, but because he DIDN'T BUILD IT RIGHT OR SOLID, he blows it - he gets tremendous charge-backs, people quit, he loses momentum.

It is TOUGH to build it one time, but to LOSE IT and GET YOURSELF IN A HOLE - then try to "COME BACK" is ALMOST IMPOSSIBLE.

Keys:

No. 1 - Build with "greenies."

- DANGER in hiring INSURANCE-LICENSED PEOPLE.
- DANGER in hiring OVER 150 MILES.

No. 2 - Give your recruits enough personal attention.

- Recruit ONE-ON-ONE across the kitchen table.
- Every recruit MUST be FIELD TRAINED a minimum of THREE TIMES.

No. 3 - Don't let any person sell anything but MILICO insurance and FANS investments.

- No casualty insurance, stock brokers, AMWAY, multi-level, etc.
- No hospitalization, medical, credit life, etc.
- No license with ANY OTIIER INSURANCE COMPANY.

No. 4 - Everyone starts on "the same level" as rep and has the same opportunity to move up.
No. 5 - Don't let anyone use our sales force.

- Nobody EVER uses A.L. Williams sales force to sell anything
- Nobody EVER comes into A.L. Williams and OVERRIDES our sales force for their leads, referrals, clients, gimmicks, nothing!
- NEVER a replacement or compensation of any kind from a referral including playing games with reassignments.

No. 6 - Build it The A.L. Williams Way. Follow A.L. Williams principles, traditions, guidelines, etc.

It is worth "PAYING THE PRICE" to "DO IT RIGHT" the first time. Don't lose your opportunity by TAKING SHORT CUTS and doing dumb things!

Use your "common sense ..."

How to Always Stay Motivated

"You must always be a winning example."
—Art Williams

No. 1 - Keep doing the same things you did as a District Leader.

- Recruit
- Field train
- Build leaders

No. 2 - Don't let negative people, losers, people who disappoint you, and rejections destroy your attitude.

(Always be positive)

No. 3 - Understand that people's negative attitudes are caused because -

---

- They aren't winning
- They don't believe they can win
- They quit

No. 4 - You must always be "a winning example." (You always "do it" first.)

No. 5 - You must have local success before your people believe. (Not good enough for just company leaders to win.)

No. 6 - You must have your priorities in order. (A lousy spiritual, personal and family life equals a lousy business life.)

No. 7 - You can't tell your people what you think most of the time - can't lose patience. This is an endurance contest.

No. 8 - Don't let your overrides dictate every decision.

- Do what's right
- Honor your commitments even if it costs you
- Your REPUTATION is everything

No. 9 - Be tough.

- Want to quit - But can't
- Get tired - But can't rest
- Believe - when everyone doubts

No. 10 - Don't mess with your people's money.

- Don't sell anything to your people
- Don't charge your people rent, fees, etc.

No. 11 - Work hard.

- Hard work makes up for mistakes
- Build with a series of 90-day commitments
- Always keep prospecting - Builds mental toughness

No. 12 - The key to maintaining an exciting atmosphere:

- Keep 'em coming and going
- Pass NEGATIVES UP and POSITIVES DOWN

No. 13 - Contact someone every day and thank, congratulate and motivate them ... (Don't wait - You will only discuss problems if you do)
No. 14 - Make your people feel good and special.

- Always give compliments
- Look for the good things in people

- Ask your people their opinions and input
- People want to feel loved and needed.

No. 15 - Expect your people to succeed.

- You run an RVP factory
- You sell hope and opportunity
- Be an eternal OPTIMIST

No. 16 - Have the guts to let your people make mistakes. (You learn by doing)

No. 17 - Forget your mistakes.

- All you can do is all you can do
- Nobody's perfect

No. 18 - Treat your people good.

- Don't threaten and intimidate
- You might not like a person, but be good to him

No. 19 - Build strong personal relationships. (You must live with your people through good times and bad times)
No. 20 - Burn all bridges and make a total commitment.

- You won't ever be average and ordinary again
- Total commitment brings happiness and purpose to your life.

No. 21 - Build with the right kind of people.

- Greenies
- Use the A.L. Williams Profile

No. 22 - Don't over-promote or oversell. (Tell it like it is.)
No. 23 - Get to know the spouse. (Really care about your people.)
No. 24 - Be a good person and be loyal (You can't fool your people very long.)

No. 25 - Always sell "the Dream." (Everyone want to be somebody.)

No. 26 - Don't worry about things that might happen ... (99% of the things you worry about never happen.)

No. 27 - Tough times don't last ... but tough people do. (Don't show hurt and don't show quit.)

THE PARTNERS IN A.L. WILLIAMS

IN THIS SECTION:

- The Partners in A.L. Williams
- Priorities of Partners
- Keys to Building
- Characteristics of the Partner Leader
- Dangers to Avoid: The Spouse
- Dangers to Avoid: The Licensed Person
- Married RVPs and Managers
- The Single RVP /Manager
- Partner Leaders Strive to Provide
- Keys to Building for Partners
- Male Partners

The Partners in A.L. Williams

"Most companies call them spouses, we call them Partners and they are truly a part of the team. Their efforts are recognized ... whether directly or indirectly involved in the business."
—Art Williams

Partnership in A.L. Williams has two aspects:

No. 1 - First, and of most importance, is the personal partnership.

- Partners who love and respect their husbands/wives will want to share goals and will try to show helpful, enthusiastic, positive attitudes. These attitudes include:
  - Giving the licensed Partner the freedom to give this business a try

  - Making the home front free from turmoil and conflict (in other words, a happy place to come home to)
  - Giving the licensed Partner moral support (being their biggest "booster")
- Partners who have an understanding attitude will usually get involved in as much "helpful" activity as they can ... activity which helps that licensed Partner in any way possible to do his/ her job better and with more ease, whether that activity be:
  - In the home or where the family is concerned
  - In the office or in administration/paperwork·
  - Licensed and working in areas that would aid financially and help relieve pressures

  (The various ways to support or lend a helping hand in these above areas is limitless and one area of support cannot be considered more important than another. The Partner does what needs to be done according to the personal circumstances.)

No. 2 - The second aspect of Partnership involves activity which moves beyond helping the wife/husband exclusively.

Naturally, anything the Partner does to build and support the husband/wife individually affects everyone in the organization. It involves activity which helps people in the organization, particularly the Partners.

- Building a business in A.L. Williams involves working with and building people. This means helping those people to achieve their goals ... providing instruction, motivation, communication, recognition and challenges for growth to that end.
- At first this effort to work with people in your group can be a one-on-one effort, and a Partner's effort can consist of two or three Partners who join together for a common purpose.
- The overall plan and purpose for the Partners Group must always center around the philosophy of helping the individual from the standpoint of:
  — Helping spouses be more comfortable with A.L. Williams, the company and the people
  — Helping spouses understand the company, its products and its philosophy
  — Helping spouses stay informed and up-to-date on company news
  — Helping spouses find answers to questions they might have

- — Helping spouses become committed to their Partner's goals
- — Helping spouses stay motivated and encouraged
- — Helping spouses understand the importance of their support now
- — Helping spouses recognize the contributions they can make in the future
- — Helping spouses develop leadership abilities and find their talents
- — Helping spouses grow with success as their Partner grows

Priorities of Partners

The company has stated its philosophy of priorities of God first, family second, and business third. The priority to the family is husband/wife, then children. (Working in A.L. Williams should never jeopardize the family needs or the husband/wife relationship.)

- The first and primary priority to the family and to that Partnership in A.L. Williams is doing what your husband/ wife needs and wants you to do.
- Priorities change with circumstances.
  - For a time, a major emphasis might be working a full-time job or being in the A.L. Williams office. For others, it might be taking care of a family of growing children.
  - A priority list will have many items on it, and some items near the top today will be at the bottom tomorrow and a year from now new ones will appear.
- In a Partner's list of priorities, every Partner needs to consider "responsibility to the people they bring into this business."
  - Although the licensed Partner may be the one who actually did the hiring and training, the unlicensed Partner's effort, even in small, seemingly insignificant ways, can make a dramatic difference.
  - Working with the people in the organization (Partners in particular), is something the Partner gradually grows to appreciate and will want to include in her/ his priorities.
- Managing everything on the Partner's list of priorities can be difficult and challenging. It involves

a maturity and realization of one's capacity for growth just as your licensed Partner is more and more able to cope with the increased demands of a growing business. One aspect of a Partners Organization is the tremendous support and helpful ideas that are shared.

Keys to Building

Attitude and Commitment

No. 1 - You can't begin too soon!

- Sales Leaders, District Leaders, Division Leaders, Regional Managers and Partners need to begin efforts toward building and reaching the Partners. This is not something that should be postponed until the RVP level.
  - Both husband and wife should be present at all three stages of the sales process.

  - Both husband and wife should understand completely the "buy term and invest the difference" concept.
- This effort begins at initial "recruiting," when the licensed person comes into the business. The spouse needs to be reached then.
  - Both husband and wife should understand the opportunity. It doesn't matter which one does the business, they both need to make that initial commitment. And, they both need to evaluate and renew these commitments on an ongoing basis.
- A proper orientation through meetings or lots of one-on-one time is needed for the spouse as well as the licensed person.
  - Spouses are encouraged to be present at all A.L. Williams meetings. It will be impossible to attend every single meeting, but they should want to be there.
  - There should be opportunities in every organization for the spouse to be a part of a Partners Organization and attendance at Partners meetings should be encouraged.

No. 2 - It's never too late.

- No matter what the circumstances have been for not developing an active Partners group in the past, it can begin now.
- No matter what the size of your organization or the distance between your people, or the seemingly insurmountable task you might face, it can be done.
- No matter what your attitudes have been in the past, it's not too late to change that.

No. 3 - It takes time and effort and it takes a leader.

- It could take a year just to get things moving. Once you make the commitment. you don't quit.
- It takes time to build it right, just like building the business. People and personal relationships aren't developed overnight.
- It takes effort. It won't happen by itself. Continued effort must be put forth to make things happen. Always remember the only way to never make a mistake is to never do anything. Take action, do something, even if you do make mistakes.

- It takes a leader. A Partners group just does not continue to grow and develop without a leader at the top ... someone or some group everyone can look to and follow.

Characteristics of the Partner Leader

The leader must have the right attitude.

- The leader(s) must have a primary motivation to reach out and help the spouses find success in this business as it relates to them. The purpose is not to help you, but for you to help them!
- The leaders of the Partners group are not in competition. They don't do what they do to seek recognition, or to gain production, business-wise. They do what they do for the purpose of helping other Partners. (If you do things for the right reasons, good things in the way of recognition and more success in the business will eventually come to you.)
- The leader(s) must have an attitude of love and caring for everyone. Every spouse should be

made to feel comfortable and important, and a part of the group. The leader avoids and discourages cliques.

- The leader(s) must understand the responsibilities of leadership, by providing example, encouragement and direction to those spouses in their organization.
- The leader(s) should learn not to take things personally. (If you let one person affect you or hurt you, it upsets all of the people.) Bearing up positively under criticism or temporary troubles is part of the mantle of leadership.
- The leader shows enthusiasm for what she/he is doing. Being the leader is fun, not a burden.
- The leader has patience in "delegating" and working with people. It is easier to do the work of 10 people than to get 10 people working, but the benefits and growth, in the latter instance, are unlimited.

Dangers to Avoid: The Spouse

Don't overwhelm the new spouse with too much.

- Some spouses need a period of time to learn and to deal with their concerns in a friendly, supportive atmosphere. Just concentrate on being a friend initially.
- Don't try to "sell" the negative spouse. Let them meet and get to know you as a person first. Let them ask questions. Be genuinely concerned about their families.
- Commitment to become involved usually comes with time. "Working in the office," "organizing meetings," "doing things to help in the business," can be intimidating initially.
- Don't tell the spouse she/he must be licensed and must help recruit, etc. This is a personal preference that a small percentage will want to do, but the percentage of Partners directly involved in the sales side of the business is small.
- Help your Partners to determine their individual "comfort zones" in A.L. Williams.Don't expect them to fit "a mold;" allow for individual differences.

Dangers to Avoid: The Licensed Person

Don't say the following to the licensed person:

- "For you to succeed, your spouse has to be involved."
- "A. L . Williams expects. .. "
- "You can build your business twice as fast if you get your spouse working, too."

Instead, say:

- "We want to meet your wife/ husband."
- "I'm sure your wife/husband will want to know what this is all about, and I want to sit down and talk with her/him about this. When can we get together?"
- "We are having a Fast Start School/ Orientation Meeting, and this is the time we ask all husbands and wives to attend together. We'll come and pick you both up."

- "We'll be introducing you both to the RVP in our office on ...."
- "In A.L. Williams, you will be working toward building your business. It's like a family business in many ways. If you make it a full-time career, your spouse will play an important part."
- "We have a Partners Organization in our office and your wife/ husband will want to come out and meet will be calling ________ (Presenting the Together Toward Success brochure to the spouse might be good at this point in time.)

Married RVPs and Managers

No. 1 - It begins with you personally.

- The example you set in your personal life, as husband and wife, is critical.
- How you share and work this business together influences others.

- The encouragement and position you give your wife/husband sets a standard.

---

*No. 2 - Your wife/husband needs to participate with you in the business.**

- Tell them you need them.
  - Make a list of things you need and delegate something to them.
  - Find something for your wife/husband to do that she/he feels comfortable handling.
- Compliment their efforts and give them credit.
- Expect some rejections and excuses, but don't give up. It takes time to develop a cooperative, growing partnership.
- Expect frustrations, but work through them together!
  - Be prepared for input and evaluation from your spouse. Their interest and concern are normal.
  - Realize that you both will be dealing with many of the same pressures and demands.

No. 3 - Give your spouse specific directions that involve working with others.

- Keep your request specific and simple. (Example: "Call Cindy and get to know her." OR "Get joan, Mary and George to come over this week and all of you plan a family picnic.")
  * This does not mean being involved in recruiting or in sales.
- Keep changing your requests. (Remember, you're the leader in this area as well as in the business side.)
- Gradually, provide more demanding opportunities for personal growth and leadership. (The greater the challenge, the greater the growth.)
- Encourage your wife/husband to implement the "Steps for Partners" in your organization.

No. 4 - Spend time with the spouses in your organization.

- Try to get to know personally the spouses of any of your personal recruits.
- Establish an "Orientation Meeting" for the Partners in your organization or meet with both husbands and wives together for orientation.
- Be available to answer questions.·
- Speak at the Partners meetings from time to time.
- Provide the Partners with opportunities to know you and have confidence in you as a leader.

No. 5 - RVP/Manager must be the person to encourage spouse participation.

- For the spouse to come to meetings, the licensed person must be the one to go home and encourage that spouse to attend these meetings.
- The Partners must be recognized by the RVP / Manager when the licensed Partner is recognized. (Example: Partner name included on plaques, Partner receives similar awards with the licensed Partner, such as t-shirts.)
- RVP/Manager must establish a recognition program for the top Partners in their organization.

(Example: Partner of the Year, Partner's Hall of Fame, etc.)

No. 6 - RVP /Manager should be familiar with how a Partners Organization should function.

(See "Keys to Building for Partners")

The Single RVP/Manager

No. 1 - Study the last three sections for the married RVP /Manager, which also apply to all single RVPs and Managers.

- Spend time with the Partners in your organization.
- RVP /Manager must be the person to encourage Partner participation.
- RVP /Manager should be familiar with how a Partners Organization should function.

No. 2 - Select one spouse (or couple of spouses) to provide special leadership for your Partners group. There must be someone responsible.

- Tell them you need their help.
- Meet with the Partner leaders regularly to give them input and motivation.
- Give your Partner leader(s) specific directions that involve working with other .....
  (See "Giving Your Spouse Specific Directions")
- Have them report to you, for your approval, their plans for meetings and other activities.

No. 3 - Rotate your spouse leader periodically.

- Have this understood in the beginning. Ask this Partner leader to help you for a specific period of time (next six months or year) OR for a specific job (i.e ... organizing a particular meeting or event.)
- Watch for their situation to change and for yours to change as well. (You have the advantage of choosing your Partner leader.)

Partner Leaders Strive to Provide:

No. 1 - Partner leaders provide good communication.

- Leaders don't assume others have all the news and information they have. Leaders share everything they know and they make it a point to stay informed.
- Leaders feel a responsibility to stay in touch on a regular basis.

No. 2 - Partner leaders provide recognition.

- Leaders want to tell others when they are doing a good job, when they are succeeding, or growing in any area.
- Leaders want everyone to feel special in their unique way, and will look for opportunities to praise everyone, but will also hold up individuals as extraordinary examples of success.

No. 3 - Partner leaders provide challenge for growth.

- Leaders believe that each person has special talents and abilities that are innate but that the potential of the individual in many areas of personal development is enormous, if not limitless.
- Leaders provide opportunities to give people experiences that will stretch them to new heights of personal growth.
- Leaders help others overcome their fear of new and challenging experiences.

No. 4 - Partner leaders provide instruction.

- Leaders see that every aspect of A.L. Williams products, philosophy, the way of doing business, and pertinent news and information is explained to Partners.
- This doesn't mean that, as the leader, you have to know every detail. What it means is that you see that instruction is provided and you have a basic understanding.

- Instruction doesn't take place at one Orientation Meeting or one Fast Start School, but is an ever-growing experience.

No. 5 - Partner leaders provide motivation.

- Leaders motivate by their attitude and activity.
- Leaders provide insights and direction that help others cope with challenges.
- Leaders master the art of building people up and making them see themselves as special and capable of achieving their goals and dreams.
- Leaders are motivated personally, and are positive, excited people at all times.

Keys to Building for Partners

No. 1 - Try to get spouses to A.L. Williams meetings.

- Do your part in contacting new spouses.
- Stay in touch and motivate those who have been there to keep coming.
- Provide special reasons for them to come. (Examples: Come to hear special speaker, help with the event, take a special part in the meeting, enjoy something special that's been planned for Partners and families, etc.)

No. 2 - Develop a "core" group of Partners.

- Build a close personal relationship with two or three Partners in your organization.
  - Pick people you relate to best.
  - Ask your husband/wife who the key people are who you should get to know.
- Invest the time and effort to make strong friendships with these people.
- The success of a Partners Organization is not how large it is in numbers or the numbers of meetings you have, but rather how successfully you carry this "core group" effort downline as your group grows.

No. 3 - Develop a plan.

- Let this "Core" group participate in all planning.
  — Share ideas.
  — Share responsibilities with them.
- Determine the needs of the Partners in your organization.
  — Set goals and keep them simple.
  — Do first things first. (Example: Meet people, communicate, be involved in activities which support the management team, etc.)
  — Announce your plans/ goals.
  — Evaluate as you go.
  — Study and use the Partner materials that are available in the A.L. Williams Distribution Center (Partner's Pack, Steps for Partners, MALE Support Team Booklet, Best of the Best, etc.). These provide a wealth of "how-to's."
- Don't quit!
  — Remember that this takes time.
  — Your Partners group grows at the pace of your organization's growth. (The commitment of the Partner grows with the commitment of the licensed Partner.)

No. 4 - Do things unrelated to the business.

- Find some time to go to lunch, share a common interest, visit a home, extend a helping hand, show a spirit of concern and love.
- Build strong personal relationships through sharing all aspects of your life.

No. 5 - Develop a team spirit.

- Always look for special talents others can share.
- Involve as many people as possible.
- Let everyone know you need their help.
- Give opportunities for people to volunteer.
- Learn the art of delegation. (This helps to insure the growth of your people.)
- Try to make everything fun.

No. 6 - Communicate with the spouses in your organization on a regular basis.

- Telephone, write letters, send newsletters and office bulletins to the home on a regular basis.
- Share all the information you receive. Don't assume other Partners have access to what you know.
- Make use of current Partner materials in the A.L. Williams Distribution Center.

No. 7 - Show special appreciation to the spouses for their efforts and positive attitude.

- Remember simple "thank you's."
- Implement regular recognition for your Partners along with the recognition given the licensed spouse.
- Establish a traditional awards program for the spouses (Partner of the Year, Rookie Partners, Up and Coming Partners, etc.).

No. 8 - Plan meetings for Partners.

- Schedule meetings when your group of Partners becomes too large to handle one-on-one.

- Try to have most of your Partner meetings and activities coincide with other A.L. Williams meetings. (For example: Partners meetings held on Client Night would be only for partners of those new recruits who would be there; a management Partners meeting would be at the same time that management meets; Fast Start Schools, Partners meetings would be at Fast Start School weekends, etc.)
- Don't have meetings unless they are needed, but remember that periodic meetings are needed just to get every Partner together for motivation.
- Establish the purpose of any meeting.
  - Plan sessions to accomplish specific goals.
  - Provide speakers from A.L. Williams' Partner ranks and management ranks and provide discussion for learning and sharing which centers ONLY around business-related concerns and business-related activities they are involved in.
  - Everything must relate to A.L. Williams.
  - Provide an opportunity for building personal relationships and a team spirit among the spouses.
  - Provide opportunities for building leadership qualities and personal growth.

- Characteristics of a successful Partners meeting:
  - Provide a friendly, enthusiastic atmosphere, one that encourages participation for all and makes the most reluctant or newest person feel welcomed and important.
  - Share A.L. Williams personal stories of success.
  - Deal with topics of frustration or concern that Partners have and share ideas toward positive solutions.
  - Provide A.L. Williams information.
  - How to succeed
  - Company concepts and philosophy
  - Overview of company news and technical information
  - Ideas on spouse involvement
    (The list goes on ....)
  - It's very important to provide a time for questions and discussion. (Having a meeting which involves good discussion and sharing personal stories of success are the two most critical aspects of a successful meeting.)
  - Plan recognition of some kind at every meeting. (Small gifts, ribbons or name tags, even the simplest forms of recognition count.)

- Evaluate your meetings according to the above guidelines and always strive to make them more interesting.

Male Partners

No. 1 - Provide male Partners with company information.

- Make a special effort to get them to A.L. Williams meetings.
- Make all news, motivation and materials available to them.
- See that they have copies of the Male Gram, MALE Support Team booklet and tapes (available from the A.L. Williams Distribution Center).

No. 2 - Include male Partners in your Partners program.

- Seek out the male Partners and get to know them one-on-one. Invite them to be a part of what's going on.
- Recognize their attendance at the meetings.
- Make a point to include them in discussion.
- Invite them to speak on the program. (Try to have at least one male Partner speak at your Partners meetings.)

No. 3 - Recognize special male Partners.

- Include them in your Partner recognition program.
- Look for leaders among the men and assign them responsibilities involving male Partners.

No. 4 - Provide a special meeting time for male Partners to break away from the general Partners session.

- Give them an opportunity to meet and get to know other men who are part of the MALE Support Team.
- Give them an opportunity to share concerns and frustrations and ideas that provide positive results regarding their role in A.L. Williams.
- Encourage participation of male Partners in the A.L. Williams National Fraternity and the formation of local chapters. (See MALE Support Team booklet and tape for specific guidelines.)

Remember, as the number of female RVPs grows, the male Partner is becoming an increasingly visible and important part of the Partners organization. Your role as as leader is to make sure male Partners feel welcomed, accepted and appreciated as a vital part of your support team, that their role as a supportive and sharing partner in

A.L. Williams is very important and that this is a family business where they can have a tremendous impact.

BUSINESS PRINCIPLES

IN THIS SECTION:

- Business Principles
- Intent Is What Counts
- Our Product Philosophy
- How We Develop Our Products
- Invest the Difference in An IRA
- Leadership vs. Management
- Husband and Wife RVP Teams
- Protect the A.L. Williams Sales Force
- Do It Right - Securities Sales
- Code of Ethics
- The A.L. Williams “Promise” to You

Business Principles

"I believe that A.L. Williams is a great company because it's a good company. We will never lose our commitment to do what's right."
—Art Williams

I made a COMMITMENT to every person on February 10, 1977 when A.L. Williams was born:

No. 1 - We will never hold anybody back.
No. 2 - We will never deny anyone an earned promotion.
No. 3 -You can pass up and earn more money than those over you when you join A.L. Williams.
No. 4 - We will help you and be there when you need us (you won't be alone - we are a team).
No. 5 - We will give you everything you need to win.

No. 6 - We will never ask you to slow down. You can always earn more and build it bigger if you want to.

No. 7 - We will never embarrass you when it comes to dealing with the consumer - we will always "do what's right" for the consumer.

No. 8 - We won't wait for you.

No. 9 - We won't beg you.

No. 10 - We won't quit with you.

This has been "THE FOUNDATION" upon which the A.L. Williams company was built.

As I look to the future of A.L. Williams I see only two things that could really DEVASTATE our GREAT COMPANY:

Recruiting the wrong kind of people that would take advantage of our freedoms and our opportunity

RVPs not building "the A.L. Williams Way," not following our PRINCIPLES AND TRADITIONS

I PROMISE the A.L. Williams company and all our A.L. Williams people:

I AIN'T CHANGING and A.L. WILLIAMS AIN'T CHANGING.

I WILL OUTLAST THOSE WHO WOULD TAKE

ADVANTAGE OF US. I WILL BE HERE LONG AFTER WE GET RID OF THEM.

I believe you can be ULTRA SUCCESSFUL in business and still do WHAT'S RIGHT.

A.L. Williams has proven that A.L. Williams is a company you can believe in.

I hope we can always count on our people to STAND UP for the REAL A.L. Williams in all their business activities.

Intent Is What Counts

"We expect our people to have a dedication to always doing what's right. There's just no other way to build a great company."
—Art Williams

We try to have very few rules and regulations, but we expect our people to use COMMON SENSE.

There are some "greedy" minds out there who can't think of anything but themselves; we've built a "me" generation in America, made up of people who want to win only for their own benefit.

These people will use the goodness of A.L. Williams to further their own profits.

If you are the kind of person who can't put the rights of others before your own, can't succeed without stepping on other people or using other people - you are not going to make it in A.L. Williams. You aren't good enough for this company.

We want to leave a LEGACY in this industry of being good, honest and sincere people.

Our Product Philosophy

"We believe buy term and invest the difference is the greatest concept available today for income protection and savings potential for the average income family."

—Art Williams

No. 1 - It meets the needs of families for more protection at a lower cost.
No. 2 - A.L. Williams sells term 100% of the time.
No. 3 - Our people sell what they believe in owning on their own lives.
No. 4 - We sell one product.

Most companies have a ratebook that's one inch thick; our ratebook is one page thick. The consumer can't stand a fence-sitter. Most companies have dozens of products and if you don't want one, they will sell you another. At A.L. Williams, we sell what we think is best 100% of the time.

No. 5 - We believe that cash value insurance is a flawed concept.
No. 6 - Cash value life insurance has three major weaknesses.

- The "bundling" concept - your insurance and your savings are "lumped" together in one vehicle.
- You pay a premium for three things: protection, investment and retirement - but you can only

exercise ONE of these elements at a time - NOT all three.

- The cash values are owned by the insurance company - NOT BY THE POLICYHOLDER!

No. 7 - The ultimate goal is to become financially secure.

The ultimate goal for "buy term and invest the difference" is to enable our families to control their own futures.

Provide the amount of death protection really needed to protect the income at a time when needed the most.

An individual controls his savings.

Accumulate enough savings to eliminate the need for death protection.

No. 8 - Our product philosophy is based on "the theory of decreasing responsibility."

The "theory of decreasing responsibility" shows the wisdom of the term insurance choice. You need a lot of coverage in the early years, when your responsibilities and expenses are high. You need less protection in later years, when responsibilities and costs have decreased.

You buy low-cost term in the early years, then "invest the difference" in a promising investment program. You have protection when you need it in the early years and cash from accumulated savings in the later years when you need cash.

MOST COMMON MISCONCEPTION ABOUT LIFE INSURANCE: That life insurance is a "permanent" need each family has. The "theory of decreasing responsibility" shows that life insurance is a way to protect your family by "buying time" until your personal financial estate is in order. Once you've built a cash estate, your need for insurance greatly diminishes.

How We Develop Our Products

"At A.L. Williams, we base our products on the needs of the average American family."
—Art Williams

When we develop our product, we always consider three things:

No. 1 - Always first - It must be good for the consumer.
No. 2 - It must be good for the salesperson.
No. 3 - It must be good for the company.

Why term has not been popular in the past:

- Consumer
  - Didn't like level term with increasing premiums
  - Didn't like decreasing term with level premiums
  - Didn't like temporary term
  - Didn't like expensive term
  - Available in the marketplace ONLY if tied in with a whole life policy
- Life insurance people didn't like LOW COMMISSIONS!
- Life insurance company didn't like POOR PERSISTENCY or POOR PROFITS.
- Our term product solves those problems!
- Our product has:
  - Level term, level premium
  - Protection to age 85
  - Guaranteed rates

- Guaranteed renewability
- Flexibility
- Highly competitive rates
- Volume discounts
- Good commissions
- Good profits

• How have we done this?
- Developed a huge system of independent business men and women
- Offered an UNLIMITED business opportunity
- Built a mass distribution sales force utilizing the part-time agent concept
- Eliminated company expenses for maintenance and training of sales force which do not have to be passed on to the consumer
- No advertising expenses which have to be passed on to the consumer
- Reduced administrative cost
- Average industry administrative cost is 7 employees per every $100 million administered - MILICO's administrative cost is LESS THAN ONE employee per $100 million administered.
- Latest in computer technology - fully automated systems
- Modernized underwriting requirements

— Simplified products
— Streamlined management concept

Invest the Difference in an IRA

"The IRA is the perfect match to the term insurance concept."
—Art Williams

- The IRA is the most perfect investment vehicle available to Middle Americans.
- Everyone who pays taxes should have an IRA. (The qualified IRA has the complete approval of the federal government.)
- You should never invest in any kind of savings or investment program until you have put the MAXIMUM AMOUNT ALLOWED INTO AN IRA.

The IRA Gives You Two Distinct Advantages:

- IMMEDIATE TAX ADVANTAGE - you take $2,000 (earned income) per working spouse

($250 non-working spouse) "OFF THE TOP" of gross income, and possible tax rate as well.

- LONG-TERM TAX ADVANTAGE- You defer tax on the contributions and the interest earned to the IRA until you begin withdrawing funds during retirement.

Choose to either the invest your money in an IRS or send a check to the IRA.

Buy Term and Invest the Difference in an IRA is the best concept available today!

Great Vehicle for an IRA for Middle America Is a Mutual Fund:

- Investing the difference in a mutual fund is one of the best investment concepts for middle American families.
- **With mutual funds:**

---

1. You become an OWNER, NOT A LOANER.

Suppose you invest money at a bank in the form of a Savings account You deposit the money and, in return, receive 51/2 or 6% interest. Most people believe this is a very "safe" investment. But, here's what happens. After you invest your money in the bank, the bank lends it out or invests it directly into the American economy. The bank receives a high rate of interest on its investment and is happy to pay you a low 51/2% for the use of your money.

---

2. You get the benefit of PROFESSIONAL MANAGEMENT.

Mutual funds invest the money of their shareholders. These funds are managed by professionals, an advantage normally available only to the wealthy.

---

3. You get the benefit of DIVERSIFICATION.

A mutual fund's portfolio is well-diversified. By owning many different stocks and bonds, the mutual fund can reduce the impact of one poor selection and offer lower risk than investing in one or two stocks.

---

4. You get the benefit of "pooled resources."

Most people don't have a large lump sum of money to invest. They have to start off with small amounts or monthly contributions. Mutual funds represent thousands of small investors - as well as large investors- who "pool their money" to get the advantage of large money resources and professional management.

5. You get the benefit of a great track record.

Mutual funds have a great track record. According to the "Weisenberger Investment Companies Service Management Results," covering the period ending December 1984, the average long-term growth mutual fund appreciated 398% for the 10-year period ending December 31, 1984. Many mutual funds represent conservative investment vehicles with a good safety record.

Leadership vs. Management

"The only way to lead is by example.
The cardinal rule of leaders should be to never ask anything of their people that they haven't done themselves."
—Art Williams

No. 1 - We want our leaders to "do it" first.

Everybody and every company talks a good game. W' e want to show people how to win by being a PERSONAL EXAMPLE. Our leaders must have a "do it first" attitude.

If you want people to sell, you sell first. If you want people to recruit, you recruit first; if the competition rears its head, you be the most aggressive - show your people how it's done. Don't just TELL your people what they should do, SHOW them! BEFORE YOU TELL YOUR PEOPLE ANYTHING, SHOW THEM WHAT YOU HAVE DONE.

Our leaders WORK FOR THEIR PEOPLE: their people don't work for them. We don't believe in "employee/employer" relationships.

No. 2 -We believe in a concept called 'Pushing Up People."

The only way you can succeed is by attracting other great people and helping them to succeed. You can't succeed by yourself.

You can't put your success before that of your people. For example, you should never have a contest where your people get YOU a promotion. You should help them to get THEIR promotion.

In turn, their success will "PUSH YOU UP."

No. 3 - We believe in treating people right.

We NEVER manage or lead with threats or intimidation. We lead only by personal example

People are skeptical - and they should be - they've been tricked and hurt often enough.

To succeed, you must be the kind of person people respect - honest, sincere, genuine and caring.

No. 4 - Before you can become a leader, you've got to become a great person.

Live by the principles you "TALK."

Live the kind of life you want people to follow. Take care of your family, take care of your financial security (make money and save money), achieve your goal of financial independence, sell by "personal example."

No. 5 - Don't try to overpromote the opportunity.

The biggest problem with our company is that our opportunity sounds too good to be true.

Our opportunity is INCREDIBLE- you never need to

overpromote it. It speaks for itself and is unbelievable on its own merits.

Learn to relate the opportunity to people's situations. Don't show them a MILLIONAIRE IF THEY'RE A TEACHER OR A COACH: They can't relate to that.

Show them an example of success that they can relate to and understand.

The Greatest Part Time Opportunity in America

A few reasons to work part-time with A.L. Williams:

No. 1 - It's a challenging job.

- You must earn your license.
- Everyone can't qualify.

No. 2 - We don't just sell policies.

- We save people money.

No. 3 - You can help people.

- "Buy term and invest the difference" is the best concept available today.

No. 4 - You can begin to build your own business.

- You work for yourself- you're your own boss.

No. 5 - You learn something worthwhile.

- Learn the keys to making money work for you.
- Improve your own family's financial planning.

No. 6 - You can earn more money than at other part-time jobs.

- One sale a month may give you an extra $100, $200 or more.

No. 7 - Practically No Risk. All you pay is small licensing fee.

Husband and Wife RVP Teams

"We never want to put a husband and wife in competition with each other."
—Art Williams

A.L. Williams permits both the husband and the wife, as individuals, to become reps or RVPs, if that's what they want.

BUT, A.L. Williams STRONGLY recommends ONE RVP per "team." A.L. Williams believes that partners should WORK TOGETHER to build a business.

Both partners come out better in the long run this way.

Why?

No. 1 - Easier To win Contests ...

Many A.L. Williams trips, meetings, conventions and so forth are based on CASH FLOW figures. If an RVP had a spouse working in the business and was overriding that spouse at LEVEL 1, that couple would have a better chance of "winning" or qualifying for the trip than an RVP who had a spouse who was a "district" or a "division." Remember that the OVERRIDE is GREATEST at LEVEL 1.

And that couple would be MUCH better off than an RVP couple competing in the contest, since there would be NO OVERRIDE situation between husband and wife (see policy #3 below).

No. 2 - Less Competitive ...

Sometimes earning your RVP promotion is simply a matter of "pride.·· A.L. Williams understands that. It IS a GREAT ACHIEVEMENT to make RVP. But A.L Williams has also learned, from experience, that there may be increased "competition" between husband and wife if both are building regions.

If it is a matter of pride and self-esteem with a

spouse to "MAKE IT" to RVP, then that spouse should GO FOR IT and earn his or her RVP promotion. THEN both partners would build separate regions and run separate businesses.

BUT ... be aware that this couple would have a GREATER CHANCE in contest competition if one of the spouses RETURNED to LEVEL 1.

Policy Regarding Spouse Licensed and Working in the Business.

1. No reason for spouse to get licensed unless he or she plans to solicit for sales or service clients. Then, MUST have license in insurance and/or securities. Rep's spouse must report to the same RVP.
2. Below Regional Manager position, the spouse can NOT be counted as a management "leg" toward promotion, and he or she can't be a "replacement" toward promotion.
3. At RVP level, RVP can't override a spouse who is an RVP.
4. HOWEVER, working toward the RVP level, the licensed spouse production would count toward $10,000 submitted production requirement for RVP promotion.

5. When the "2nd spouse" reaches RVP, the spouse will be coded RVP under the same upline RVP and then the husband and wife will each build separate regions.

'Guidelines "2" and "3" are to PROTECT the A.L. Williams system from people who might get their spouse licensed and then assign people to that spouse to increase overrides.

Circumstances to Avoid

- Competition ... ("My" organization vs. "Yours"; who produces the "most," who gets the "most" recognition, etc.)
- Conflict in leadership ... (Husband/ wife disputes on how to run the business; people in the organization not feeling one leader but two and constantly being confused on whom to follow.)
- Conflicts in loyalties ... (husband/wife loyalty and interest being to their people rather than each other.)

Who is assigned an organization in the event of RVP death?

It depends. In most cases, the company automatically reassigns people to the upline RVP.

HOWEVER, when and if there is a licensed spouse who has proven capable in sales and management, and could provide the kind of leadership the organization would need, then A.L. Williams would consider assigning that organization to him or her.

A.L. Williams WOULD NOT reassign an organization to a spouse who has simply been a "figurehead" RVP or leader, with no actual ability or practical experience in the business.

A.L. Williams makes these decisions based on what is best for ALL concerned.

Protect the A.L. Williams Sales Force

"As A.L. Williams and its leaders become more successful and well-known, there are many who will try to join A.L. Williams 'to take advantage of us!' I consider it one of your 'Top Priorities' to protect the A.L. Williams sales force."

—Art Williams

Guidelines and "things to avoid"

- Avoid people who want to use our sales force to "MARKET" other product
- Avoid people who want to "SELL" things to our sales force- "PRODUCTS" "LEADS," "REFERRALS," etc.
- Avoid people who want to use your name or position as an "IN" to our sales force
- Every A.L. Williams person "LICENSED ONLY" with MILICO and FANS
- Recruit and build with "GREENIES":
  - Be CAREFUL with INSURANCE LICENSED PEOPLE.
  - Everyone STARTS as a TRAINING REP- no exceptions.
  - Every new recruit observes A MINIMUM OF 3 FIELD TRANING SALES.
  - Use A.L. W1LLIAMS GUIDELINES ONLY for promotions.
  - BUILD WITHIN 150 MILES - BELOW RVP level WITHIN 50 MILES.
- RVPs are EXPECTED to be "full-time," "devote 100% of their business lives" and "be a POSITIVE, WINNING example" for A.L. Williams.

An RVP (you must make a full-time commitment to be an RVP) may never "go back part-time" and still continue to override his region as a Regional Manager.

- Never loan your people money. Help them by giving them your support and leadership. Loaning money does not solve the problem.

Grounds for termination, suspension, demotion or other discipline

Violators can be terminated, suspended, demoted or subject to other discipline for the following:

- MISHANDLING MONEY
  - — Endorsing reps' or managers' checks and stealing their money; they earned it.
  - — Stealing licensing money; NEVER have a separate "licensing account."
  - — Selling promotions and/ or people; our people earn their promotions honestly - they don't buy a contract.
  - — Not paying bills; hurting A.L. Williams' reputation.
  - — Putting leases, bills, financial obligations in A.L. Williams' name. Should be in individual RVP's name.

- Taking advantage of your people
  - Regional Managers and below NEVER pay any expenses, rent, fees, etc. (immediate termination).
  - NO A.L. Williams person makes a "profit" from his people for supplies, fees to meetings, use of company computers or from RVP "clustering " (immediate termination) .
  - A.L. Williams people make money ONLY by selling our products and overrides from building an organization.
- Selling life insurance with any company but MILICO
- Selling investments with any company but FANS
- Selling any products except those authorized and approved by A.L. Williams
- Less than full-time effort by an RVP ... or not actively supervising the total organization
  - RVPs can't relocate base shop without permission of NSD or Art Williams.
  - RVP can retire under Estate Plan only as fully qualified SVP.
  - RVP must be a leader in production and recruiting.
- Not complying with A.L. Williams replacement policy

  - When replacement is taken, it is FINAL. No additional replacement even if original replacement fails."
  - Never take a replacement from a new recruit over 150 miles.
- Playing games with A.L. Williams guidelines, rules, contests, ethics, etc.
  - Reassigning people for promotions
  - Signing sales to win contests
  - Intimidating and threatening your people
  - RVPs must honor commitments to their people.
- Violating any insurance or securities regulations - such as:
  - RVP signing insurance application sold by unlicensed insurance person
  - Unlicensed person soliciting or picking up policies
  - RVP signing securities application sold by unlicensed securities person
  - Insurance licensed rep talking about securities and carrying securities sale material without securities license

- Trademark Infringement
  - — The name "A.L. Williams" and the A.L. Williams logo are registered service marks and exclusive properties of the company.
  - — They must never be used without permission from the A.L. Williams Legal Department, and should always be used in a proper and professional manner.
- Contacting State Insurance Departments
  - — Contact with any state insurance regulatory office should nor be made without approval given by the A.L. Williams Compliance or Legal Departments.
- Misusing Printed and Audio Visual Materials.
  - — Do not duplicate, reproduce or change any company sales material without written permission from the A.L. Williams Legal Department.
  - — Only approved A.L. Williams sales, recruiting and training materials may be used for clients and recruits.
  - — Flyers, leaflets, pamphlets or mass handouts cannot be used in any way. (ie: no flyers on car windshields, house-to-house leaflets, passing out cards on the streets, etc.)

  - Only exceptions: Company-approved referral letters and "Common Sense" return postcards, which may be inserted into copies of Common Sense.
  - Only newspaper ads approved by A.L. Williams Home Office may be published and then only by an RVP.
  - No video or audio taping of any A.L. Williams meeting for distribution - only taping for personal use is allowed.
- Terminations
  - Only A.L. Williams, Inc. can terminate an RVP.
  - NSDs, SVPs and RVPs recommend termination
- Contacting the media
  - No one should represent A.L. Williams to any news media, newspaper, radio television or any form of mass communication without contact and approval from the A.L. Williams Public Relations Office.
- Pressuring clients
  - A.L. Williams representatives never sell on the first visit.
- Misrepresenting A.L. Williams
- Help "POLICE" A.L. Williams sales force:

— REPORT ANY VIOLATORS to NSDs or Art Williams

A.L. Williams is positioned to PAY OFF BIG for our leaders. I PROMISE you I won't let anyone WHO DOESN'T BELIEVE IN and IS NOT COMMITTED to A.L. Williams "PRINCIPLES AND TRADITIONS" hurt our great company and our FABULOUS future.

Do It Right - Securities Sales

"It is important that each of us understands the importance of handling our securities business correctly."

—Art Williams

Consider the following examples of actions taken by the NASD against people from other firms:

No. 1 -

In March, 1984 a person without a securities license was caught soliciting mutual fund sales using prospectuses and sales literature. He was fined $25,000 and is banned from association with any member of the association in any capacity.

No. 2 -

In August, 1983 a person "failed to properly discharge his supervisory responsibilities." That person had unlicensed securities people under his management who were giving prospectuses to clients. He was fined $5,000) and suspended for six months and was required to requalify by examination.

At A.L. Williams, any non-securities licensed person carrying security sales literature, prospectuses or any non-securities licensed person in any way soliciting a sale for mutual funds will be terminated, as well as that person's immediate manager.

Also, the RVP is subject to termination. Example: If a non-securities licensed sales leader is giving out prospectuses, the sales leader and the district leader will be terminated and possibly the RVP!

No. 3 -

In February, 1984 a person with a securities license, who was not present at the sale, signed a mutual fund application that was written and sold by a non-securities licensed person. The licensed person who signed the application was fined $36,000 and banned from association in any capacity. The immediate supervisor was fined $20,000 and banned from association in any capacity. The non-securities licensed person who solicited the sale was fined $25,000 and banned from association in any capacity.

At A.L. Williams any person who signs an application and is not present at the sale will be terminated as well as the upline manager with the RVP also subject to termination.

At A.L. Williams any non-securities licensed person taking an application for securities will be terminated as well as the immediate manager and the RVP will also be subject to termination.

It is important that we do it right at A.L. Williams. It is not worth your career to do things the wrong way. **If in doubt, don't do it!**

Code of Ethics

A.L. Williams management believes that a business, in order to exist and prosper, must always consider the human factor and place a high value on the individual. A.L. Williams is built on strong personal relationships, based on true, honest friendship; we believe that this type of organization will succeed far better than one based on business relationships alone.

A.L. Williams management recognizes that an individual can only reach full potential in a company environment that offers opportunity, encouragement and recognition, and that fosters individual initiative. It must be an environment that allows each person to be "the best he can be."

A.L. Williams believes in service to the consumer, including fair and proper analysis of the client's financial needs, careful and honest presentation of our product, and dedicated follow-up service and concern.

A.L. Williams selects its leaders based on their morals, character and ability to deliver. This company will be led, through positive influence, by people doing what is right and living up to their commitments.

The leaders of **A.L. Williams** will manage by

example. They will be fair-minded and objective in all their activities. A.L. Williams people will never manage by intimidation, excessive rules or threats. They will always strive to do what's right for their own people and for the public that they serve.

A.L. Williams believes in considering the family unit in all of its internal business practices. The company's commitment to family is total and unfailing. A.L. Williams will always welcome the spouses of representatives and leaders into all business functions and activities. A.L. Williams is a family business.

A.L. Williams believes that for a person to be his best, he must be a total person. with life's priorities in the proper order. We believe that order should be spiritual life, family life, and business life.

A.L. Williams management believes that in order for people to achieve the greatest success in an organization, they must maintain a total commitment to its philosophy and procedures, and must put their total working efforts into the business.

We believe that the company is obligated to match the commitment and dedication of the individual with the company's total support and commitment. A.L. Williams will always support its people.

The A.L. Williams "Promise" to You

- We will give you THE "BEST" PRODUCTS in our industry to sell to your clients.
- We DON'T sell by using PRESSURE, TRICKS or GIMMICKS.
- We make our clients feel COMFORTABLE. We DON'T sell on the FIRST INTERVIEW and we DON'T talk down to people and make them feel INFERIOR.
- We give you a COMPANY with a PHILOSOPHY. We believe in "Buy Term and Invest the Difference." WE SELL what we believe in owning on our OWN LIFE.
- We sell TERM LIFE INSURANCE 100% of the time. American people are tired of people who won't take a stand - "fencesitters."
- We DON'T sell just POLICIES. If we can't save you money on what you have now or give you more value for your dollar, we don't deserve your business.

- We will give you a POSITIVE, ENTHUSIASTIC and EXCITING COMPANY. Most American companies are worried, hurting and crying. A.L. WILLIAMS is SUCCESSFUL, HAPPY and BREAKING ALL PREVIOUS RECORDS.
- We will give you the BEST PART-TIME OPPORTUNITY in America. it is possible to make a LOT OF MONEY doing a GREAT JOB for people.
- You will feel GOOD about the job you do for people.
- You will NEVER be REQUIRED to give up the security of your full-time job. You can stay part-time FOREVER at A.L. Williams.
- We will give you HOPE and OPPORTUNITY again. Give you the chance to DREAM again.
- We will give you a chance to OWN YOUR OWN BUSINESS - The American Dream.
- We will NEVER DENY you a PROMOTION when you QUALIFY.
- We will always let you EARN MORE and BUILD IT BIGGER - if you want to.
- We will give you an opportunity to PASS UP and MAKE MORE than those ABOVE YOU and those who have been HERE LONGER than you.
- We will give you a company that's CONTROVERSIAL. Any NEW IDEA meets resistance.

- We will give you a chance to be a member of a NATIONAL CHAMPIONSHIP TEAM. We are at the top of our industry.
- We will give you a chance to FEEL GOOD about YOURSELF: to become SOMEBODY.
- We will give you a chance to become a REGIONAL VICE PRESIDENT - to be your OWN BOSS.
- We will give you a chance to IMPROVE YOUR LIFE FINANCIALLY. A chance to become TOTALLY FINANCIALLY INDEPENDENT.

FINALLY - We will give you a chance TO TAKE CHARGE OF YOUR LIFE AGAIN.

Made in United States
Orlando, FL
21 December 2024

56313344R00241